LIBERAL DEMOCRACY IN NON-WESTERN STATES

LIBERAL DEMOCRACY IN NON-WESTERN STATES

Edited by

Dennis Austin

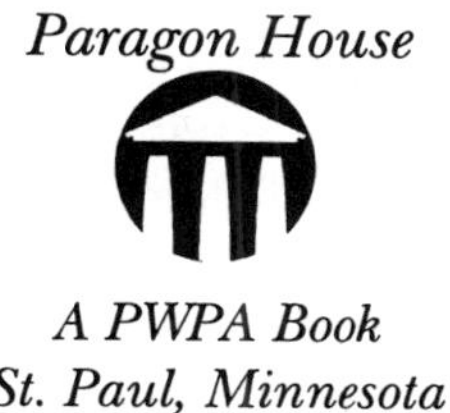

Paragon House

A PWPA Book
St. Paul, Minnesota

Published in the United States of America by
Professors World Peace Academy
2700 University Avenue West
St. Paul, Minnesota 55114

A Professors World Peace Academy Book

The Professors World Peace Academy (PWPA) is an international association of professors and scholars from diverse backgrounds, devoted to issues concerning world peace. PWPA sustains a program of conferences and publications on topics in peace studies, area and cultural studies, national and international development, education, economics and international relations.

Library of Congress Catalog-in-Publication Data

Liberal Democracy in non-western states / edited by Dennis Austin
        p. cm.
      "A PWPA book"
      Includes bibliographical references
      ISBN 0-943852-98-6 (hc.) — ISBN 0-943852-99-4 (pbk.)
      1. Developing countries—Politics and government.
      2. Democracy—Developing countries. I. Austin, Dennis, 1922-   .
JF60.L53   1995
321.8'091724—dc20   92-3014
                                                               CIP

TABLE OF CONTENTS

Liberal Democratic Societies

SERIES EDITORS: ROGER MICHENER AND EDWARD SHILS

Civility and Citizenship
EDWARD BANFIELD

Morality and Religion
GORDON L. ANDERSON AND MORTON A. KAPLAN

The Mass Media
STANLEY ROTHMAN

Nationality, Patriotism and Nationalism
ROGER MICHENER

Work and Employment
DAVID MARSLAND

Democracy in Non-Western States
DENNIS AUSTIN

The Balance of Freedom:
Economy, Law, and Learning
ROGER MICHENER

Liberal Democratic Societies is part of a larger series on World Social Systems by Morton A. Kaplan, General Editor. The other systems examined are the Soviet System, series editor Alexander Shtromas, and China, series editor Ilpyong J. Kim. These books are available from:

PWPA Books

2700 University Avenue West, Suite 47
St. Paul, MN 55114, USA
Phone (612) 644-2809 • Fax: (612) 644-0997

SERIES EDITORS' FOREWORD

Liberal democratic societies, as patterns of political, economic and social arrangements, would seem to be vindicated against their detractors. Until recently Marxism in its various forms and other proponents of single party states and centrally planned economies appeared to offer realistic and allegedly beneficial alternatives to liberal democracy. Events in China, the Soviet Union, Eastern Europe, and the Third World have so reduced the persuasiveness of these arguments that there are no readily apparent alternatives to liberal democratic societies.

Nevertheless, the discomfitures and embarrassments of single party states should not be regarded as a justification for complacency. We should be appreciative of the merits of liberal democratic societies, but we should be aware of their shortcomings, in light of their own ideals, and of the dangers to which they are liable.

The purpose of the present series of books is to take stock of and to assess, in a historical perspective, the most central achievements and shortcomings of liberal democratic societies, and to encourage thought on their maintenance and improvement.

Not only do we seek to delineate some of these main lines of historical development of the variant forms of liberal democracy, but we also seek to discern certain fundamental postulates that are common to these institutions and processes. In this way, we hope to define more clearly the liberal democratic ideal and its limits. We wish to learn where the practice falls short of the ideal or deforms it. We wish to form an estimate of the destructive forces within the liberal democratic ideal itself and of their potentialities for causing its deteriorization or its collapse. We wish above all to learn how these destructive potentialities may be averted.

This series insists on the bond between liberalism and

democracy. Liberalism and democracy are two distinguishable components of present-day liberal democratic societies. Their combination into a particular form of society is a great achievement but it is also a source of difficult problems. For instance, can these societies reconcile the fundamental conflict between minimizing governmental authority and intrusiveness and the democratic demand for more governmental activities and greater governmental provision of welfare services? What are the consequences of some of the institutions of liberal democratic society for the daily life of the individual in his or her private sphere? These questions and others like them constitute a continuing challenge for the present and successor generations. These books are devised to assist in the understanding of that challenge.

Roger Michener
Edward Shils

PREFACE

Dennis Austin

> *La dernière chose qu'on trouve en faisant un ouvrage,*
> *est de savoir celle qu'il faut mettre la première.*

The chapters which follow this brief introduction are the revised papers given to the panel on 'Prospects for Liberal Democracy in the non-Western World' as part of the 1989 London conference on *Liberal Democratic Societies: their present state and future prospects*. A delay in publication has been useful since it allowed some account to be taken of the remarkable sequence of events in what was formerly the USSR. The picture today is very different from that of a few years ago. The demise of communist rule in Russia, together with the weakening of Marxist-Leninist beliefs across the world, have left the western democracies in the ascendant and, flattered by imitation, they have been willing to believe that they can be imitated. Is it a justified or a mistaken belief? The questions addressed by those who submitted papers to what was a very agreeable meeting under the auspices of the Professors World Peace Academy, turned on whether in fact the present community of democratic nations is likely to be enlarged not only by former Marxist states but other non-Western countries.

LIBERAL DEMOCRACY IN NON-WESTERN STATES

There has always been a handful of Third World governments with a claim to be called democracies. (They are discussed in subsequent chapters.) Over the years, the position changed from time to time. Some were destroyed by military junta or single party dictators; others returned to a qualified form of democracy. In the current wave of reform, very many states have begun to move away from authoritarian rule to a more tolerant style of government, although there are still those, notably China, which are under harshly autocratic regimes. The kaleidoscope of reform is constantly changing and there is, unfortunately, no political barometer to enable us to foretell the future climate of good and bad government, only a mixture of declared intentions and actual achievements. And it is the confusion of motives and results, under very difficult circumstances, which forms the substance of later chapters.

What do we mean by liberal democracy? When looking at the transfer and adoption of democratic patterns of control, a distinction has to be made between the copy of institutions and an acceptance of political values. The former may be lifeless, the latter may exert a strong local appeal, although not every non-Western government has been responsive to the charms of elected parliaments and civil liberties. Façade democracies have begun to appear which hide their brutality behind an appearance of reform.

Should we draw a distinction between democracy and liberal democracy? That democracy, *tout court*, has its adverse side is well-known. Its promotion of a vulgar commercialism, and its embrace of mediocrity, is evident from our present (Western) surroundings. But there have been deeper worries. There has always been the danger that democratization will enhance the power of the state rather than the local citizen, that it will centralize and not disperse power, and uphold the equality rather than the liberty of individuals. It is to temper such proclivities—abetted during our own century by socialist philosophies which saw the state as a distributive agent—that democracy needs its liberal counterpart. It needs the liberalism which emphasizes the importance of civil rights, and of what has become known as political participation by men and women as free and active citizens who are equal not simply before an all-powerful state but in liberties safeguarded by a constitutional government.

Through such phrases one can see the lineaments of a liberal as well as a democratic society. Its attributes are easily noted. They include a freely elected parliament, not all of the same party, a tolerant respect for opposition and for rules of the game under constitutional laws, an independent judiciary, a public service free from bias, an unrestricted press, no torture, no arbitrary imprisonment, no state seizure of property, no restraints on public meetings or on the dissemination of news, no *führer princep*. They are ideals laid up in a parliamentary heaven but they provide a pattern for the imperfect world of would-be democratic societies, and the papers printed in this volume should be seen as a preliminary attempt to assess the likely success or failure of states whose governments have begun to introduce reform or are faced with the task of maintaining those already in place.

Liberal values are not, of course, the only *desiderata*. There are ideals which others share, of unity, efficiency, order and security. In addition, all societies today, whether democratic or non-democratic, pursue the secular grail of economic growth, and democracy is likely to be judged not only by its merits but its performance. Some account, therefore, had to be taken of the relationship between political reform and economic freedom—a liberalization of markets and the spread of local wealth to match the dispersal of political power. Alongside John Stuart Mill and Alexis de Tocqueville one sees the image of Adam Smith, more emblematic perhaps than substantial, but raising problems of economic as well political change:

LIBERAL DEMOCRACY IN NON-WESTERN STATES

> The Scottish Enlightenment's notion of a 'commercial society', with the alleged benefits accruing from a free market in goods and services, has dominated the imaginations and the rhetoric of neo-capitalist movements. Even when the importance of constitutional reform has been given priority, there has often been a hidden premise that such reform was necessary to create the conditions for economic growth. (Larry Siedentop, "Tocqueville's Challenge to Liberalism," London, *T.L.S.,* Oct. 11, 1991.)

In practice, political and economic reforms have gone together and it is never easy to say which had the priority. No society becomes democratic without pain, no state achieves economic growth without struggle; and between the two pursuits, governments are as confused as policies are contorted. There are some who are prepared to adopt political reform in order, as they hope, to secure economic growth; others want economic development to underpin democratic institutions; but many wish the marriage of both—a prosperous democracy as a measure of a fairer, more equal society: one man, one vote, and a chicken in the pot for everybody. The instrumentality of political change as a means to redeem society from its poverty is certainly a recurrent aspect of the accounts given later, but it is also clear that, for many within the former Marxist states and the Third World, democracy has its intrinsic value which it would be ungenerous to dismiss as economics dressed as politics. Society wants it, and leaders must grant it.

How greatly the world has altered! Fifty or more years ago, western democracy was threatened by totalitarian regimes which then exerted their own baleful influence. Today, the reverse is true. Dictatorship is under challenge from democracy. So the whirligig of time brings in his revenges, but for how long? There is neither permanence nor certainty in political fortunes. We need to remember what has always been the case, that the ground recovered from dictatorship by democracy may one day have to be regained. In the meantime, however, the hope of reform is running strongly and it is the task of this book to try and measure its achievements.

CHAPTER 1

O BRAVE NEW WORLD?

Dennis Austin

Early in the morning of Friday, August 24, 1991, a small group of men, cheered on by onlookers and armed with acetylene torches, ropes and hammers, began to demolish the statue of Felix Dzerzhinsky—founder of the Soviet state security policy—which had stood as an icon of fear and authority in front of the KGB Moscow headquarters. Down came the huge statue, hacked from its base, and down came the central structures of communist rule—the party, the KGB, the central presidium, the post of General Secretary, the party newspaper, *Pravda,* together with the property and wealth which they controlled. All were changed, changed by the loss of power and privilege accumulated over 70 years of communist rule—an extraordinary reversal of history, as dramatic (though far less violent) as the overthrow of the tzars. An ideology of government which had hoped to revolutionize the world had been abandoned. The Union of Soviet Socialist Republics has ceased to exist, and no one is sure what to put in its place.

If one tries to assess the impact of western parliamentary democracy on the rest of the world, where better to begin than with the astonishing demise of Marxist-Leninist beliefs? The current hope in Moscow is still that of democracy and market reform through perestroika, society set free under constitutional laws and free elections, and the morass of the economy transformed by imitation of western capitalism. What better tribute can there be to western practice? If, against present evidence, the communist chrysalis can truly turn into—well, into something more free than its caterpillar past, a huge addition will be made to the liberal world of democratic states.

That the tide of democracy is still running can be seen from several states in the non-western world. It is almost the only current of ideas publicly endorsed by Third World leaders and their opponents, with one significant exception—nationalism—which is discussed later. Military men are uneasy in office. Single party presidents are defensive. Revolutionary leaders are on the run. Theocracies still exist but the emirs, ayatollahs and sheiks of the Middle East are not wholly at ease, even within the Islamic world: they, too, must be careful to court popular support. One must pause before the immensity of China where communist beliefs are still upheld, but the elderly leaders in Peking, at least to outsiders, look something of an anachronism, unwilling to change and fearful of survival.[1]

Hail to the demos! Yes, and one can measure its success not only in political terms but economic benefits. The capitalist engine of prosperity has worked away to lift western economies to new levels of wealth, and the neat symmetry of argument—disperse political power under constitutional laws, spread economic power through free markets—brooks no challenge. Monopoly control is seen as both illiberal and inefficient. Privatize the economy, therefore, and pluralize the polity. Who can doubt but that the attraction of western wealth has added immeasurably to the imitative value of western politics across a widening spectrum of regimes whose leaders have had to respond to an upsurge of popular discontent.

2

Why should one feel cautious, then, about the prospect of success for democratic government in the world beyond the West? There are four broad areas of misgiving, one political, another economic, the third social and the fourth, nationalism. In a sense, they cover one general ground of doubt, namely, whether liberal parliamentary democracy can adapt to local needs and work to advantage under conditions very dissimilar from those in the countries of its origins.

POLITICAL WORRIES

One line of argument comes from the writings of Michael Oakeshott. It links representative democracy to the distinctive history of Western Europe and (some) of its former dependencies, a history shaped by events not found in conjunction beyond its shores—classical antiquity, Christendom, the Reformation, the Enlightenment, the industrial revolution and the ferment of philosophical ideas which moved to and fro among contrary beliefs about the nature and purpose of the state, society and individual. Over the past two centuries, arguments which stressed the merits of constitutional politics and representative institutions gave powerful credence to the slow growth of what became democratic government, but success came from practice not from theory. Democracy has never been a transferable blueprint for political control but simply the name given to a style and form of government evolved out of experience. One is tempted to say, first the practice, then the description, and what now exists is the outcome of a particular history, the sum of established habits embedded in laws and institutions. Because western democracy has been home-grown, formed by local circumstances, it has taken different shape in Britain, Europe, North America and Australasia but these are kindred varieties, whereas to seek to transfer their beliefs and habits to an exotic soil will always be difficult. One might as readily try to plant an oak in a plant pot under conditions not native to its growth. Perhaps one might succeed for a period in grafting western democracy onto a different historical stock of beliefs and experience but the likelihood of its not taking will always be great.

The danger, therefore, is to expect too much of what might be called political or constitutional engineering since, in reality, the success of democratic institutions has been organic not mechanical. They work only if they can live and grow in the common acceptance and rooted affection of the community from which they take their form.

There is an interesting parallel in the fate of what used to be described as tutelary democracy under colonial rule. The concept was usually derided, not only because its intentions were distrusted but because of its insistence on time—time to adjust new institutions and procedures to societies whose political habits were dissimilar. It is now possible, however, to understand why, when constitutions, parliaments, parties and elections were constructed almost overnight in the rush to independence, they failed. They failed from artificiality and, for that reason, were unable to cope with local problems of political control.

One must add that they often failed because they were rejected. Liberal democracy is not to everybody's liking, least of all those on whom it imposes restraints of office. To be acclaimed by those who wish to pay homage is music to the ear of politicians, but to lose power by popular vote or after a fixed term of office strikes a very different and discordant note. Politicians then begin to suborn the constitution, corrupt the voting system and muzzle their opponents. They seek to entrench themselves in power, fearing that any change of regime is likely to insist on the need to punish past misdeeds as a necessary base to the new politics of reform. Although the wish to bury the past may also be there, the capacity to punish is indispensable to the restoration of justice, and governments which fear retribution will do everything they can to avert it.

THE HOPE OF WEALTH

The point can be made simply. A market economy has now become the reverse side of the coin of political freedom, in much the same way as political reforms are beginning to be seen as essential for economic development. The two are said to be inseparable. But suppose the adoption of an open economy does not succeed? Worse still, suppose that living standards deteriorate, as presently throughout the former USSR, under the burden of reform? The danger then is that both will be rejected—political freedom along with the free market.

The coupling of market liberalization with democratic reforms has become not only a creed but a packet for export, not so easily tabulated as parliaments, elections, freedom of debate and a list of civic rights, but broad and detailed enough to sustain a growing volume of advocacy. Within the general description of a market-led economy are specific recommendations—privatization, convertible currencies, unrestricted markets and the freeing of the economy from state control. The sweep of argument can be forceful: democracy and capitalism, the free movement of people and free movement of goods, no restrictions on public debate, no restrictions on trade. Such are the new formulae for political stability and economic growth, the golden keys to modernization in the closing years of the century.

If there is a hint of mockery in these descriptions it is to try and counter the dogmatism of a new creed. In reality, we do not know the formulae for economic growth. The dictum that democracy fits comfortably with a mixed economy is convincing, as is the belief that democracy is most easily safeguarded when the economy is not only growing but broad based in its rewards: the doubts arise over the necessary relationship between the politics of liberal democracy and the economics of sustained growth. There are historical pointers *against* the connection. A century or more ago, European economies which had begun to industrialize turned to the state, an authoritarian state, to protect and advance their interests. Free trade was seen as the biased advice given by governments whose economies were dominant. Bismarck's Germany was certainly not democratic; it was autocratic and interventionist, and it was extremely helpful to its infant industries. In recent years, the newly industrializing countries of the Far East (South Korea, Taiwan, Hong Kong, Singapore, Thailand) have been both autocratic and fast-growing. As in prewar Japan, the politics are harsh, but each has moved through a critical stage of development, and who can say whether that has been despite or because of their politics?

The problem is now recognized at different levels. Mr. Attila Karaosmanoglu, when vice president for Asia at the World Bank, acknowledged "that the East Asian NICs and their successful emulators are a powerful argument that a more activist, positive governmental role can be a decisive factor in rapid industrial growth. An urgent task . . . is to perform more research into East Asian approaches to trade and industrialization, including the experience of Japan. What is replicable and transferable must be brought to light and shared with others."[2] The admission is important. Approval of a 'more activist, positive government' not only erodes the doctrines of the free marketeers but challenges the belief that democratic government, of a hands-off disposition, is the necessary complement to economic success. The more likely assumption is that different stages of economic growth respond to different policies. Others, however, have gone farther. They have questioned whether political reform is compatible with economic development. "The relationship between development and democratization," writes Gordon White in his essay on China, "is an ambiguous one and China's current aim of comprehensive market-oriented economic reform would best be served by the maintenance of strong and authoritarian political control."[3]

Such arguments are the reverse of the belief that political and economic reform must go together, but there is no certainty either way. The record of Latin America and a number of African countries is ambiguous, except that the spiraling down of the economy, whether from a middle or low base of growth is likely to sour relationships whatever regime is in power: public resentment is directed equally against autocrats, soldiers and elected politicians. The danger in linking economic and political reform is that when one goes sour, the other suffers. If, therefore, democratic institutions are seen primarily (like Joseph in Egypt) as providers, there will be a hostile reaction at popular, as well as elite levels, if they do not deliver the goods. The point is all the more poignant since the record of most non-western countries over the past decade has been one of economic decline. They are worse off today than they were a decade ago, and if it is the case that bread without democracy is bitter, it is also true that democracy without bread is fragile.

And there is a further worry, akin to the uncertainty discussed above, namely, whether the requirements of a free market—whether beneficial or not—can be met, or even understood, where there has been no previous experience of its operation. For market structures to succeed there needs to be a broad class of business skills, market-aware entrepreneurs, local networks of supply and distribution and a political understanding of capital markets. A privatized economy is no easier to grasp in all its diversity than a democratized polity. Many non-western societies are deficient in such skills, and not the least troublesome aspect of the advocacy of 'democratic capitalism' is the sight of international civil servants and economists traveling the world in order to urge bewildered governments to adopt policies that are, in essence, the effect of a slow accumulation of experience in the western world. There is also the obstacle of governments which have as decided an interest in directing economic policy as they have in controlling other aspects of national life.

SOCIAL ILLS

Non-western societies may have sources of political health which are now unknown to the West—the cohesion of village life, fealty to local rulers, strong family loyalties, a sensibility towards the changing seasons. But many also have to bear a weight of social problems in the form of ethnic rivalry, urban poverty, political corruption and a failure of public services which oppress the ordinary citizen. Corruption saps the central institutions of government, violence is used not only in protest against the state but by the state in its reaction to criticism, and entrenched social hierarchies of caste and class are nonetheless repressive for being traditionally accepted.

Look at the worst case: a country where the boundaries are ragged and crisscrossed by refugees, some trying to escape, others looking for asylum, where a narrow ruling elite sees the state primarily as plunder, where the urban population—almost beyond control—has doubled or trebled in number, and where farmers seek to escape the predatory grasp of the government by withholding their produce from market, a state plagued by civil war sustained by imported weapons and abetted by foreign interests. Its politicians may now talk of democracy, but they continue to behave brutally and incompetently.

Is the picture exaggerated? Yes, for those Third World states where the hope of political reform is a recurrent theme, despite sustained periods of military rule or autocratic party government. But there are also states so impoverished and torn by civil conflict as to push all prospects of even the beginnings of democratic government beyond the horizon of hope. The list is long—Afghanistan, Burma (Myanmar), Cambodia, Chad, Ethiopia, Haiti, Iran, Iraq, Mozambique, Rwanda, El Salvador, Sierra Leone, Somalia, the Sudan—states, particularly within the African continent, where political life is governed by an "absolutism moderated by armed rebellion. The weakening of state authority rarely brings in its wake a plural civil society but more often warlordism based on access to hard currency and patronage over the allocation of firearms."[4] The criticism is harsh but not unwarranted when one looks at Zaire where, despite demands for change, the likelihood that any form of democracy can be established for the huge country is remote. President Mobutu may fall, Mistah Kurtz may be dead, but the horror will live on. States pushed to the edge of collapse by internal factions may recover from civil war, often remarkably, as in countries as diverse as China, Russia, the United States, Nigeria and Lebanon, but they do not easily turn to democracy once the conflict is over across the Islamic world from Iran to Algeria. A religious nationalism offers outlets for mass emotion but has nothing to do with liberalism or the democracy of civil rights.

NATIONALISM

The ethics of nationalism are ambivalent, lying somewhere between patriotism (admirable) and chauvinism (deplorable) but the appeal of nationalist sentiment is at least as strong an emotional force as liberty or democracy. Because modern democracy needs the nation-state as a legislative framework, and because nationalism is often associated with popular rights, the two join forces from time to time; but one must ask, freedom for whom? For the individual through democratic rules and institutions, or for the group through national self-determination?

There are other dilemmas. Without the unifying bond of nationhood, there can be no citizenship, and one might suppose that the dignity bestowed by being a citizen would be favorable to political equality. Yet the record of nationalism throughout the present century has been atrocious. In the West, it has been one of aggression between states and oppression within its own frontiers. In many non-western states, it has not been a unifying but a disruptive force, particularly where there are strong ethnic rivalries. One would have to go back to the naivety of Woodrow Wilson to believe that national self-determination is a democratic process. Were

God and His angels to rearrange the human map of the world to give each person a true habitat, one might still fear that political ambition and local jealousies would foster discontent among ethnic groups, subnationalities, tribal enclaves, religious sects, and regional interests, each with its separate loyalties and defining shibboleths.[5]

Western democracies, among them states which once exceeded the worst atrocities of almost any post-colonial regime, now like to hold their nationalism and their religion in reserve, although Basques, (some) Irish, Catalans and Bretons are still restless. But the frailty of state loyalties, reflected in the terror imposed by rival nationalities, has drawn close again in Eastern Europe. What meaning is there to the democracy of 'one man one vote' in the Serbian areas of Croatia or disputed areas of Bosnia Herzogovina or among the Hungarian minority in Slovakia, or the Nagorno Karabakh enclave in Azerbaijan? On August 30, 1991, against a background of killings, Azerbaijan declared its independence from Moscow; on September 2, Nagorno Karabakh followed suit against Azerbaijan. The redefinition of a national self by a particular group constantly narrows its focus to exclude those who were once fellow citizens.

The problem is that we do not know how representative institutions can function in excessively plural societies. There have been numerous attempts to devise new democratic forms by establishing modes of 'consociation', but they have run into their own problems since to give special expression to particular groups via an arithmetical federation or schemes of confederation runs the risk of exacerbating, rather than softening, the animosities between them.

These are four serious grounds for reflection. They cannot be passed over. They are doubts which question whether long-established political arrangements among rich industrial western states can be introduced into non-western societies that must cope with difficult problems of national diversity, economic weakness, strong religious sentiments and a political culture shaped by different historical traditions . . . But we need to draw back a little. Too pessimistic a view divides the world, unalterably, into light and dark. On one side, Hyperion; on the other, the satyrs of the non-Western world. But such a picture is too stark. The world is not like that. There are always shades of light and dark, and it may be premature—looking at the world as a whole—to dismiss the current desire for democracy as merely imitative and therefore bound to fail.

How can one redress the balance between too great a pessimism and too easy an optimism?

One can begin by asking whether democracy must always be circumscribed by its origins? Is it not possible to say that it now enshrines values that are universal? Look at the ideal of free elections, politics restrained by law, no torture, no arbitrary laws, no monopoly of office and its rewards, an uncensored press and private property secured by law. Do not such benefits have intrinsic worth, a core value, which may be given expression in ways not copied but adapted from western practice? There has never been a fixed pattern of democratic institutions: modern governments are light years away from the direct democracy of Periclean Athens. Not even television and the charms of information technology can equate modern men and women, numbered in the millions, with the intimacy of the city-state. The West may rightly be skeptical about the degree of adaptation open to the successor republics of the USSR and Eastern Europe, whose leaders have to change not only their own ideological skin but the ingrained habits of past practice: there may be no resting place between the unity of communist repression and the disunity of nationalist republics. But other leaders and other societies have fared better. India has held, sometimes falteringly, to its own forms of democratic control against the challenge of poverty, religion and caste. Parliamentary rule in Japan rests on an excessive conformism behind often illiberal practices, but Japanese governments since 1945 have not been replicas of western democracy anymore than Japanese industrial society is a replica of western practice: *autres mouers, autre politique*—but within a framework of recognizable values to which we can cautiously attach the name, democracy. And we should not be too pure. We should not be so content with our own democracy as to be unable to accept the imperfections of others.

There is a good element of common sense in such arguments, and we must try and let the record of current reforms speak for themselves. There are—and have been—attempts to move away from authoritarian control. The trend has shifted, spread out perhaps, from Eastern Europe to Russia and across a growing number of non-western states. Some of the reforms have been induced by revolution, some by governments anxious to survive, many because of the dismal performance of the economy. Additionally, there has always been a small cluster of states which have struggled to keep a parliamentary form of government in place—Costa Rica, Malaysia, (some) Caribbean and Pacific Islands, India and Japan, Botswana in Southern Africa, Mexico and Senegal. Others have clawed their way back to more democratic, less brutal, politics after decades of military control and dictatorship—countries as different as Chile, Argentina, Turkey, the Czech and Slovak republics, Poland, Hungary, the Philippines, Namibia and South Africa. There are declared *intentions* by several one-party governments in Africa to accept a plural form of politics, as well as demands for reform across Asia from Korea to Thailand and Indonesia. The transforming power of free elections was dramatically demonstrated in South Africa in 1993-1994 under F.W. de Klerk and Nelson Mandela.

Others may not succeed. Some perhaps do not intend to succeed, although even the hypocrisy of politicians who only pretend to favor democracy is something of a tribute to its power, and governments that say they want open debate but refuse to allow it sometimes find that words can be used to compel action. Other would-be reformers have made little ground against hostile governments. The overall pattern is very mixed. At one end of the spectrum are states whose leaders set their face against any reform; and—moving away from the worst—an array of weak democracies, partial democracies, quasi-democracies and all-but-democratic regimes. One is left with a muddle, but that is not unusual when looking at taxonomies of good and bad government. There is no guide to failure or success, and it is better to do as the French advise—*il faut donner du temps aux temps*. At present, Eastern Europe, beset with economic fears, is a confused mixture of partly democratic and non-democratic regimes—the Czech republic at one end, Romania at the other. Asia—China apart—looks more cheerful than Africa. A number of South American and Caribbean states—Haiti apart—are closer to the democratic end of the spectrum. The future of Russia and the rest of the former Soviet Union is beyond conjecture: many of its leaders are eager for democratic reform but fearful of the consequences, some are local nationalists, others do not know what they want. The eventual outcome (in the phrase once used by Winston Churchill) is still 'a riddle wrapped in a mystery inside an enigma'.[6]

A further puzzle. Given the difficulties facing most non-western societies, and the different pattern of political behavior from dictatorial to (almost) democratic, can one say *why* states have moved in one direction or another? The general problems, common to most, have been discussed; but can one single out favorable as against unhelpful circumstances in which democratic institutions are more or less likely to succeed? Is the critical factor one of leadership, or resources, or social homogeneity, or ancestry or size?

(1) Size? Almost certainly not. Tyrants come large—China, as well as small—Haiti, Equatorial Guinea, and middle sized—Iraq, Iran. Democratic regimes of different degrees of virtue are similarly varied. There are democratic mice—Barbados, Malta, Mauritius, and democratic elephants—India and (less certainly because more recently) Brazil. Some small

communities, such as Fiji, have slipped from relatively democratic government into military rule; others, very large, such as Argentina, have moved in the other direction. Being small or large, island or mainland, landlocked or coastal, tropical or temperate may pose particular problems but most commentators have sensibly concluded that size of territory or number of citizens is rarely a defining factor in relation to the democratic temper of a country's politics.[7]

(2) Legacies? Of greater importance. We inherit and reshape, and myths redefine the past almost to the point where what we believe about our history, and what we remember or forget, is more influential than what happened. When circumstances become favorable, the past can be adjusted by a selective history—Goethe in place of Goebbels, Manzoni not Mussolini. But the larger legacies are not so malleable and one can detect a number of determining elements in the ancestry of most modern states.

For example, within the postcolonial world, governments, since independence, have been fundamentally influenced by their colonial past. On the debit side, French rule in Algeria and Indo-China, Belgian rule in Zaire and Rwanda, and Dutch rule in Indonesia, while over many years of an obsession with communist threats, American policies gave protection not to democratic parties but to anticommunist rulers. But where there was a sustained impress from western political ideas, and a determined effort to give local expression to their practices, the legacy has been more helpful than not. Parliamentary democracy in India cannot be understood without the absorption of ideas and habits from Britain among the English-educated middle class with its links through Congress to the ordinary voter—ideas which were, of course, used *against* British rule in the subcontinent. (The *debit* side of the *raj* was the authoritarian ethos of its rule which Indian democracy can claim to have legitimized but not diminished.) The Japanese were force-fed with American political beliefs during the postwar years of occupation. And there was a comparable if lesser impact by the West on the political culture of a number of former colonial states, the critical factor usually being the depth and duration of the impression reflected in constitutional structures and political manners.

Other legacies have been troublesome. In Latin America, the nineteenth century wars of independence against Spain were fought by national armies which are now part of the complicated equation between politicians, church leaders, large landowners and the military. How much or how little struggle there was in the achieving of independence had its effect. Too bloody a war, as in Algeria, Angola, Mozambique and Vietnam may spill over into the independence years; but too easy a transition brought its problems, as in Nigeria where self-government was ill-defined in relation to the competing number of regional and ethnic claims. In this respect, too, India was probably lucky. The long struggle for independence was fought not on battlefields but through civil disobedience, party debate, round table conferences and constitutional argument—a useful political education. That has not been true in any sense of Russia where 'overcoming the past' has been a recurrent theme in its history—and at no time more difficult than today.

(3) Leadership? In earlier decades there were newly independent governments which grasped the opportunity of favorable circumstances to maintain parliamentary structures of control and a tolerance of opposition. They included leaders as different as Nehru in India, Norman Manley in Jamaica, Tanku Abdul Rahman in Malaysia, Seretse Khama in Botswana, Seewoosagur Ramgoolam in Mauritius, Léopold Senghor in Senegal, Milton Margai in Sierra Leone and the Senanayakes in Sri Lanka—a gallery of national heroes who, by temperament and background, were prepared to govern moderately, in ideas as well as policies. (Pandit Nehru was rarely commended for his moderation—until his daughter became prime minister.) Others tolerated no check to their power and gave full reign to their appetite.

The successors to these early leaders have not done as well—Sri Lanka and Sierra Leone are steeped in tragedy—but one can point to Carlos Menem in Argentina (and other elected governments across South America), Mrs. Aquino in Manilla, Michael Manley in Jamaica, Quett Masire in Botswana, Jugnauth in Mauritius and Dr. Mahathir Mohamad in Malaysia. Their problems have been greater. The 1960s and 1970s, a time of expanding world trade, were a good deal more favorable to elected governments than the 1980s, a decade of unfavorable trade balances for many non-western economies.

What induces a president or prime minister and his followers to hold to democratic policies? Innate beliefs? Education? International pressures? Or the conjunction of politics which pose no radical threat from opposition interests? We do not know, but when one reflects on the folly of Kwame Nkrumah, the cupidity of Ferdinand Marcos, the cruelty of Idi Amin or the fanaticism of Pol Pot, quite apart from the demonic influence of Hitler, Mussolini, Franco, Stalin, Mao Tse Tung, it seems sensible to reopen the interesting debate—long derided—of the personal influence of men and women on the political direction of those under their control.

(4) Resources? As argued earlier, political reform and economic progress are linked but not twinned: there is no direct equation—'the rich are democratic, tyranny goes with poverty.' One can see how autocracy and wealth join forces in the oil-based economies of the Middle East. Indeed, if governments are very rich—Saudi Arabia and Brunei—they can hope to buy off political discontent, although to be abjectly poor, as in the Sahel countries of West Africa, is no basis for *any* government. If a general barometer of political fortunes were needed, one should probably read off the rise and fall in economic well-being rather than the actual levels of wealth or poverty. To remain democratic in adversity is a stern test but there are states—Jamaica for one—which have continued to hold elections and a party-based government and

opposition despite a declining economy. Nevertheless, when one looks at the government in, say, Malaysia one can see that it has kept its own form of parliamentary democracy, despite communal jealousies, all the more easily for being able to point to a rising standard of living from local revenues. How far better placed the new rulers of Russia would be if they could demonstrate a comparable success.

Resources matter, and their distribution as much as their capacity. The interesting cases are the 'little tigers' of East Asia. They are not top-heavy rich, as in Saudi Arabia and the Gulf states; they are manufacturers, traders, industrial producers, and it will be interesting to see whether a growing economic maturity will make the pressure for greater political reform irresistible. The signs are there in the increased support for the Democratic Progressive party in Taiwan, the merger of the main opposition parties in South Korea, and support for the opposition in Singapore and for elected members in Hong Kong prior to its reabsorbtion into China in 1997. The relationship of economics to politics, always close and never simple, cannot be quantified but it is certainly easier, other matters being equal, to be democratic when society is well endowed and prosperous than poor and destitute of resources.

(5) Plurality? The point has been made that ethnic conflict can quickly erode the national census on which democratic institutions depend. It fashions the key that unlocks all of Pandora's box save hope. Look at Sri Lanka, and how that 'Third World democracy' was dragged down to civil war by difference of language, religion, regional identities, myths of origin, external concerns and a range of issues from government employment to education and landholdings. By 1985 an Indian army was in occupation of the Tamil north, and a murderous uprising divided the Sinhalese community in the south. A list of similar conflicts needs no emphasis here; there are almost daily accounts of violence across the globe between rival communities whose appeals for communal solidarity,

couched in populist terms, demand not only justice but revenge.

Do such conflicts make democracy impossible? No. They hinder its capacity to mediate and mar its ethnic of tolerance. But one can make two points. First, that states—such as Japan—which do not have such problems, which have a high degree of social, religious and linguistic unity, came late to democracy: unity can supply dictators as readily as it can sustain democracy. Second, democracy needs to be seen as part of the problem of ethnic or racial conflict but as the basis for its solution. The case is arguable, since any assertion of the 'democratic right of self-determination' may raise demands which are then violently resisted, but when one looks at Pakistan or Nigeria it is also clear that military rule and its decidedly undemocratic measures of control offer no solution. It is true that, whereas western governments tend to stress the virtues of plurality, non-western governments fear the consequences of disunity, but if democracy cannot encompass the plurality of communal differences, what else can? The answer given by the Soviet Union was the discipline and terror of a single party, but the price paid by its citizens in labor camps and execution cells was intolerably high.

If, therefore, one is looking at ethnic factors and the survival of democratic institutions, the answer (as often in politics) must be ambivalent—most liberal democratic states can cope with some, but not too much, plurality. Democracy is certainly compatible with diversity, as may be seen in states as different as Switzerland and Malaysia; that they can also be torn apart by subnationalisms is all too evident in what was once Yugoslavia and, at a lower level of intensity, in Nigeria. India is of great importance in this respect since it stands as a test-case whether democratic pluralism can meet the challenge of ethnic and religious violence. It is, indeed, a nice question whether India can be governed at all other than through its democratic institutions of parties, parliament and constitu- tion.[8] It has the advantage of a multiple diversity of shifting alliances instead of the single divide in Sri Lanka, but still one cannot be sure whether the communal rivalry which now frightens minorities and threatens the secular basis of the state will undo the 40-year old consensus on which the Union was democratically constituted.

How perverse humankind can be! There was once an Indian guru who taught his followers from Muslim and Hindu texts. On his death, each faith claimed him as a saint in a dispute that ended in violence between the two communities.

CONCLUDING REFLECTIONS

1. The desire for democratic political reform now exists from Mongolia to Ghana, from Papua New Guinea to Ecuador, but if judgement is needed on performance, one must ask not about intentions but whether a particular regime is less brutal today—less oppressive, more tolerant, more representative and more open—than its predecessors were a year or a decade ago, and whether the movement for reform, where it exists, will continue and gather pace. The evidence of later chapters shows a number of increasingly hopeful, as well as bad or doubtful, cases within a range from harshly authoritarian regimes to near democratic. There are light and dark, but also intermediate positions. Even those which fall short of what is understood to be liberal, parliamentary democracy in the West may nevertheless be law respecting, peaceful, tolerant of (some) opposition, and with not too bad a record of civil rights.

2. Most commentators now defend the prevailing expectation that constitutional reforms and market liberalization will deliver not only democracy but democracy-plus-growth—a major change from fifty or more years ago when the imitative model was not parliamentary government but either the totalitarian dictatorships of Central Europe as architects of a new world order or the Soviet model of a planned economy under party control.

3. It is urgent, therefore, that the West should do what it can to help not only Eastern Europe and Russia but as much of the non-western world as is possible. At present, the poorest states among the poor live like squatters in the shadow of the wealthy, and noone knows how to free them from their hunger, debts or dictators, but something has to be done, through the Uruguay Round and comparable negotiations, to help the not-so-poor and those willing to introduce democratic changes. If such efforts fail, the danger is that governments under attack from newly enfranchised electorates will once again seek other models, uglier, more brutal, more threatening.[10]

4. The reason why the West should help to enlarge the community of democratic and partially democratic states ought to be a matter of self interest. The world would then be safer and pleasanter. All nations have to live together in a world drawn together by new technologies, and the extent of their cooperation will be wider and more amicable if they are closer in political outlook under liberal laws and institutions. There is no alternative to that simple truth, no easy 'delectable strand of progress' or 'translunar paradise' for one section of humanity alone.[11] And the West itself is not so flawless as to be free from censure. The richest societies, including the United States, have indefensible levels of poverty and cities which are intolerably violent. Hostility towards immigrants has begun to take hold again of some western leaders. Gross financial and political corruption has spread across the Mediterranean world. There are intractable political problems in Western Europe, where the integrating structures of Community member states struggle towards accountability but have to admit a 'democratic deficit' at the very center of their operations.

5. Both West and non-western societies might also reflect jointly on the problems which begin to face the whole of humankind, problems which arise not from the economics of poverty but the rapacity of growth, requiring the politics of restraint rather than freedom. In this interdependent world,

who has wrought the greater damage—the rich or the poor, the West or non-West? If the wealthier nations continue, as they do now, to ransack the resources of the globe, one might as well (as they say) employ a goat to tend one's garden as to believe that modern individuals, free or unfree, democrat or tyrant, can be trusted to live sensibly on the planet. If the earth is used without care, there will be no 'beauteous mankind' or brave new world for those who inherit what we despoil.[12]

6. Towards the end of a millenium, the temptation to prophesy grows stronger but we would be wise to be prudent. Consider, for example, in the context of this volume, three very different problems for whic no one can forsee the remedy. Firstly, how to heal the division of the world into rich and poor, whereby one-fifth of its citizens consume more than 80 percent of its resources. How is it to be redressed, and how can its injustice be squared with talk of enlarging the circle of liberal democratic states? Secondly, the changes which *are* taking place in the distribution of economic power are happening in areas of the world where forecasts about liberal democracy are particularly difficult, namely, among the three billion or so citizens of East Asia. We may surmise that five centuries of western dominance are nearing an end, but who can say what will take its place in a world of different legacies and cultures? Thirdly, changes will surely come from the ever increasing pace of technology. It is commonplace to argue that television has both reinforced and debased the practice of democracy, but it is much more difficult to guage the effect on governments and the voting public of the computer-based information networks whose effect, for good or bad, are beginning to take shape.

Uncertainties of this kind are not an absolute barrier to understanding—we can always weigh the possibilities—but they are bound to be a restraint to our judgement and a curb on our beliefs.

NOTES

1. Cuba, too, where Marxist control is ameliorated by an anti-American nationalism.
2. Quoted in the *Financial Times*, London, October 3, 1991.
3. Gordon White, *Democracy and Economic Reform in China*, Institute of Development Studies, Sussex, April 1991.
4. Alex de Waal, review, 'Misgoverned Continent', London, *T.L.S.*, 13 Sept. 1991. A generation or more ago, African leaders dreamed of a united continent linked by pan-African ideals. Not today. The present image is closer to that of Dürer's Melancolia, of an Africa surrounded by the discarded instruments of progress, a dejected *putto* by her side, a half-starved hound at her feet—"lapsed into a state of gloomy inaction." See Erwin Penofsky's comment on Dürer's Melancolia, in *Albrecht Dürer*, London 1948.
5. Shibboleths and discrimination are nothing new. "And when any one of the fugitives of Ephraim said, 'Let me go over', the men of Gilead said to him, 'Are you an Ephraimite?'. When he said, 'No', they said to him, 'Then say Shibboleth', and he said, 'Sibboleth', for he could not say it right; then they seized him and slew him." (*Judges, 12*).
6. Winston Churchill, Broadcast Talk, BBC, October 1, 1939. The prime minister continued: "but perhaps there is a key. That key is Russian national interest"...But what is Russian or Ukrainian or Georgian national interest today?
7. See especially, R.H. Dahl and E.R. Tufts, *Size and Democracy*, Stanford, 1973.
8. The point is also made by Professor Gupta, see below Ch.6.
9. The title chosen by James Jupp, *Sri Lanka Third World Democracy*, London, Frank Cass, 1971.
10. See the special number of *Third World Quarterly*, July 1989.
11. Michael Oakeshott on "the illusion that in politics there is anywhere a safe harbour, a destination to be reached or even a delectable strand of progress..." *Political Education*, Cambridge 1951, 28.

12. "How many goodly creatures are there here!
    How beauteous mankind is! O brave new world,
    That hath such people in't."
    The Tempest Act 5, Sc. 1.

CHAPTER 2

ISLANDS OF DEMOCRACY IN THE CARIBBEAN AND THE PACIFIC

Anthony Payne

What are the present conditions and future prospects of liberal democracy in 'small island developing states'? To raise such a question is to look not at a particular region of the non-Western world (although we will shortly consider the democratic experience of small island states in the Caribbean and the Pacific, the two parts of the world with the greatest preponderance of such states), but at a specific type of state which has proliferated within the international system since the wave of decolonization began to embrace even the tiniest imperial possessions in the 1960s and 1970s. The type is described primarily by reference to the concept of 'smallness', defined in terms of population rather than land area, and further qualified in two important senses by the notions of 'islandness' and 'underdevelopment'. For present purposes, each concept is to be understood in commonsense terms.

Such an approach begs the question whether such a category can be firmly enough identified to make the exercise worthwhile. The literature in political science which seeks to investigate the issue of small state behavior is certainly extensive. Although it has generally been more concerned with the international than the domestic consequences of smallness, the latter has not been without treatment.[1] Yet, even after much reading, the analysis of the politics of small states is still left hanging rather uneasily in the air. At the end of a recent survey of the literature as applied to the many sovereign states in the Commonwealth with populations under one million people, Paul Sutton observed that "it seems clear that we are not going to develop a theory of the small state in politics equivalent to the theory of the firm in economics," adding pointedly that "much of this has to do with the failings of the discipline of political science itself."[2] Smallness as a factor can be said to offer insights, but yields little in the way of explanation. A small state, in the final analysis, is a state like other states. Nevertheless, on a more positive note, Sutton argued that five characteristics were often attributable or closely related to small size.[3]

(1) Institutional Fidelity. In nearly every case the smaller territories of the Commonwealth emerged into statehood through the tried procedures of tutelary devolution of responsibility and the adaptation of a Westminster—Whitehall system of government, that is, a representative parliament and a political neutral civil service. Both formally in respect of constitutional arrangements and informally in respect of party systems, the basic framework has been more preserved than abandoned.

(2) Governmental Pervasiveness. Small states appeared to employ larger numbers of civil servants than other countries. Central government was often the largest employer of labor in the country and frequently the most important agency for the articulation and aggregation of demands, as well as being crucial to their settlement.

(3) Exaggerated Personalism. The significance of personality was readily apparent in virtually all cases. The positive side was the accessibility and more direct accountability of leading politicians; the negative side the vulnerability of small states to domination or dictatorship by one or two individuals.

(4) Concerted Political Harmony. Small states in general, and Commonwealth ones in particular, did remarkably well on all indices of political and civil rights. They tended to enjoy regular and frequent elections, experience regular executive transfers and suffer a relatively low incidence of civil disorder. Put the other way around, they did not figure markedly on the long list of states that practice discrimination on ethnic, linguistic, or religious ground.

(5) Pragmatic Conservatism. Very few small states have adopted radical political ideologies, preferring a careful cultivation of the center as their favored orientation. Indeed, avoidance of decision-making for fear of generating external opposition seemed to have become almost routine in some states.[4]

Reflecting on the syndrome, as set out briefly above, it can be fairly claimed that these five features present a profile of politics immediately recognizable to anyone familiar with examples. The difficult, but important, question, which is not shirked by Sutton, is to judge the degree to which smallness has shaped these prevailing characteristics. Institutional fidelity relates most obviously to the colonial heritage, although a timorousness in experimentation may derive additional impetus from considerations of size and vulnerability. Governmental pervasiveness, at least within democratic as opposed to authoritarian forms of politics, can more easily emerge in a small state, although the expansiveness of the civil service may also reflect a colonial inheritance. Exaggerated personalism is now widely accepted as a common feature of small state politics and is the most widely discussed theme in the literature. Concerted political harmony can similarly be tied quite closely to size. It is presumed that small states possess a sense of community often denied to larger entities and that, some 'plural societies' notwithstanding, they enjoy a basic consensus of values which Caldwell and others attribute interestingly to their acquisition of a "dominant European maritime culture" as a consequence of their 'islandness'.[5] Those features of size which give greater opportunity for citizens to participate effectively in decisions and to perceive a relation between their self-interest, the interests of others, and the public or national interest are also worthy of emphasis here.[6] Finally, pragmatic conservatism can be said, as with institutional fidelity, to derive from the perception that not many options exist for small states in a complex, interdependent world and that low-key, cautious political strategies best serve their interests.

As indicated at the outset, these arguments do not add up to a political theory of the small state, but they raise important comparative questions. We may look more closely at the recent political record of small island states in first the Caribbean and then the Pacific.

THE CARIBBEAN

For years the Commonwealth Caribbean seemed to be set apart from the mainstream of Third World politics. Its territories mostly proceeded to independence by peaceful, evolutionary means; coups were nonexistent and political violence rare; indeed, Britain was said by some to have left behind in the Caribbean a series of 'Westminsters in the sun'.[7] The image was always exaggerated and generated complacency in too many quarters both inside and outside the region, but it did contain a large measure of truth, particularly where representative government, as in Barbados, had a long history. The picture was profoundly disturbed in March 1979 when the government of Eric Gairy was overthrown by insurrection and the Grenadian revolution was launched under the radical leadership of the New Jewel Movement (NJM). These dramatic events broke the 'rules' of Commonwealth Caribbean politics and gave rise to another, and quite different, interpretation of the region's affairs. The democratic institutions of all the states of the region were now deemed to be vulnerable to the ambitions of small groups of determined ideologues. Leftwing politics of a sort had already surfaced in Jamaica and Guyana and seemed set, in this vision, to sweep across the Commonwealth Caribbean. The tone of the analysis was generally apocalyptic, both on the Left in welcoming the apparent trend and on the Right in fearing it. In fact, what nearly everyone misunderstood about the Grenadian revolution was that it was not the model of the future. It represented a high point in the political changes which occurred throughout the region in the 1970s, but its particular form and causation were always more exceptional than typical. A closer look at the situation in Grenada before and after 1979 is needed to develop the point.

GRENADA

Grenadian politics before the revolution were dominated by what had come to be called 'Gairyism'—the mixture of brutality, capriciousness, inefficiency and corruption by which the government of Eric Gairy ruled the island. Democratic politics in the Caribbean had always contained an authoritarian and messianic element, well encapsulated in the pioneering analysis of the relationship between the 'hero' and the 'crowd' advanced by Archie Singham in the later 1960s.[8] Gairy, a particularly flamboyant character even by local standards, was the subject of that study. During the 1950s he had successfully mobilized the black masses against the old planter and commercial elites which had traditionally controlled Grenada; he subsequently consolidated power around himself and led the island to independence in 1974. However, even by that time, his 'heroism' had begun to be tainted by financial improprieties and rough handling of all political opposition. The freeing of constraints represented by independence permitted these tendencies full rein and the panoply of

'Gairyism' emerged—the repression of dissidence via the activities of the notorious 'Mongoose Gang', the rigging of election results, the exploitation of political power for economic and sexual advantage, and the mystical embrace of 'cosmic connections' which, alone among these factors, aroused the outside world's interest in Grenada's plight.[9] By 1979 the point had been reached, in a deeply corrupted political system, where liberal democratic politics could not defeat Gairy: force or acquiescence were the only options.

This picture of political life in 'democratic Grenada' prior to 1979 is essential to an understanding of the subsequent era of revolution. When the leaders of the opposition NJM, having heard that orders had been given by Gairy for their indefinite imprisonment, made their largely peaceful insurrection, it was widely condemned by Caribbean political leaders and most other commentators as a dangerous breach of the Westminster system. In Grenada itself, however, there were few who were not jubilant: they knew that the Westminster system had been breached many years earlier. On the day after the revolution, the NJM leader, Maurice Bishop, promised that free and fair elections would be held at the earliest possible moment and nobody doubted but that they would have been easily won by the NJM. In the end, they were never held and the NJM traveled, unpredictably and largely secretly, down the road of Marxist-Leninist vanguardism. The debate about the causes of this is complex and need not be entered here. It is sufficient to observe that, like Gairy, Bishop was prepared to lock up his political opponents and limit freedoms of expression on national security grounds. A substantial People's Revolutionary Army was also built up and that eventually brought the revolution to an end in October 1983 when, following a fierce ideological dispute in the upper councils of the government, several of its members put Bishop and some of his other ministers against a wall and shot them.

The savagery of this act stunned the whole of the Commonwealth Caribbean. Within the region, it was as unprecedented.

as it was unacceptable as a means to a political end. The trauma was such that it served to legitimize the resulting United States invasion of Grenada and the subsequent re-creation of liberal democracy in the island under US political management. This latter process was tutelary in the best decolonization tradition, involving the forging of an alliance between warring center factions when it looked as if Gairy might otherwise win the post-invasion election. That election, held in December 1984, was not without its heroic side. It was, by common consent, freely and fairly conducted and represented to most Grenadians the relief of a return to the normalities of liberal democratic multiparty politics. Further elections in March 1990, contested by five parties, gave a narrow victory to the National Democratic Congress and its allies (nine seats) against eight seats for the (divided) Opposition. In fact, politics in Grenada during the last five years has been pursued in the best picaresque tradition of Caribbean micro-state life. It is as if Naipaul's literary world has come to life as one aspirant leader after another has maneuvered and plotted for control of the state, culminating at the beginning of 1989 with the sick and dying prime minister being removed as leader of the governing party but still hanging onto his office! In the process, the quality of government and economic management has been left wanting; but nobody doubts that, after several extraordinary years, democratic politics (albeit of a crude and colorful character) is alive again in Grenada.

In sum, Grenadian democracy was destabilized by Gairy. All the other remarkable events of the revolutionary period followed from this—not inevitably or predictably but, for all that, inexorably. Put simply, without 'Gairyism', there would have been no Grenadian revolution. The discrediting of democratic politics under his leadership explains the ease and the manner with which the NJM took power and sheds more light than is sometimes realized on the party's authoritarian political development. In retrospect, too, it is worth noting that there might have emerged from the revolution, if its ultimate path had not been distorted by Marxism-Leninism, a democratic alternative to the Westminster model for the Commonwealth Caribbean. In its early days, the NJM used to mount a powerful critique of "the type of democracy where people walk into a ballot box and vote for two seconds every five years," asserting that "if the people have no real say on what happens between elections, then they are still mostly powerless."[10] It claimed to want to build instead a system of 'participatory democracy', involving the wider mobilization of the people within community education and health councils, youth groups, voluntary work organizations and eventually village assemblies. These ideas were far from absurd in the context of a small island developing state and some promising early initiatives were taken before an ideological rigour stifled the experiment. However, this critique of traditional liberal democratic forms, which had also gained some currency in radical political circles elsewhere in the region died with the revolution. Ironically, one of the longer-term consequences of Grenada has been to strengthen the popular appeal of liberal democracy, as conventionally understood and operated, across the whole of the Commonwealth Caribbean.

JAMAICA

Jamaican democracy similarly came under sustained attack in the late 1970s but proved to be a more robust phenomenon than the Grenadian version, surviving its trials and ultimately emerging the stronger for the process. In the period since the introduction of universal suffrage in 1944, and continuing after independence in 1962, a competitive political system emerged whereby two parties, the People's National party (PNP) and the Jamaica Labour party (JLP), fought each other as rival electoral machines. Their respective ideological positions converged to the point where they differed only on a small range of issues, none of which threatened the overriding commitment of both parties to multiple-class, multiracial politics. A patronage tradition developed in which political support was exchanged for the material benefit of a job, a contract or even a home.[11] Thus, for all the seeming vitality of Jamaican democracy, the quality of mass involvement in politics was low. The role of the poorer ranks of the party coalitions was simply to act as an accurate mirror of mass grievances, thereby enabling politicians to devise more adeptly the techniques of symbolic and material accommodation which were the basic stuff of political control. As a system, it was far from fragile, having established firm roots in the hearts and minds of the majority of the people, and yet the fact remained that it was intrinsically vulnerable to the incursion of a form of politics prepared to articulate, rather than mask, the class and racial cleavages of Jamaican society.

The 'democratic socialist' aspirations of the PNP government, elected in 1972 and led by Michael Manley, provided just that challenge. Manley's attempt over the next eight years to modernize the social and economic structure of Jamaica generated intense class and ideological conflict and gave rise to an escalating political crisis. This came to a head in 1980 with a coup attempt in June, and widespread party political violence surrounding the October election, bringing over six hundred deaths. In retrospect, it is apparent that the democratic system of the country was under real threat in what was a highly charged situation. Yet Manley did not seek to rig the election in order to stay in power, although the PNP's defeat must always have seemed likely; the JLP stopped just short of inciting a complete breakdown of law and order, even though it had the capacity to do so and had flirted with the possibility; the Jamaica Defence Force caught and punished the conspirators in its midst; and a team of honorable and brave public servants was put together to preside over voter registration for the election. The liberal democratic structures of the country came close to collapsing, but they did not quite succumb. In the end, the main reason why they survived is that enough of the Jamaican elite—politicians, civil servants, judges, army officers and others—felt the necessary attachment to the system and were ready to display, even in times of stress, a sufficient adherence to the rules of the game for it to continue.[12]

The conduct of politics since 1980 has been characterized by what can only be described as restraint. This is not to say it was uneventful or free of turbulence, but it is to recognize that leading politicians in both parties understood how close to the brink they had come in 1980. The PNP's boycott of the snap election called by the new JLP prime minister, Edward Seaga, in December 1983 and its consequent absence from the Jamaican parliament damaged the system less than had been anticipated. The PNP called repeatedly for the holding of proper elections once the issue which had prompted its boycott—the preparation of a voters list—had been resolved; but it never sought to use its public support, as testified by its regular lead in opinion polls throughout the second half of the 1980s, to make the country ungovernable. It preferred to wait and win the next election as and when it was called by Seaga under the normal terms of a five-year parliament beginning at the end of 1983. Indeed, Manley himself was wont to say that he was more concerned with the conduct of the election than the result. In this spirit, a code of conduct was signed by Manley and Seaga on behalf of their parties in August 1988 prior to the election in February 1989. It was won easily by the PNP, thereby confirming the Jamaican tradition that no party is ever given more than two consecutive terms in office by the electorate. More importantly perhaps it passed with relatively little violence. Only 13 people were killed, which was a low figure by local standards, especially as the governing party was changing, with all the attendant implications for jobs and patronage.

Clearly, on the evidence described, the quality of democracy in Jamaica leaves much to be desired and, even as it stands, needs to be constantly protected from unscrupulous leaders, trigger-happy gunmen and ambitious soldiers. The maintenance of democracy in developing societies is hard work; but it can be said that, by and large, Jamaica has toiled effectively in its cause. Powerful forces favoring liberal democracy have been forged in the country, not the least of which is a people who have become attached to their own particular electoral tradition. The role of the elite remains crucial, especially as the first postindependence generation, largely schooled in Britain into the values of liberal democracy, is ageing and being replaced by younger men and women educated either in the region or in the United States. The latter applied especially to the Jamaica Defence Force whose links with the United States have been greatly extended during the Reagan/Seaga years.[13] Yet, for the moment, the evidence of the February 1989 election encourages the belief that the political leadership of the country, in which both Manley and Seaga must now count as men at the end of their careers, may still possess enough of the ideology of liberal democracy to want to fight to preserve its existence.

GUYANA

Guyana can be compared with Grenada and Jamaica in some respects but in others its politics and sociology are different—but not, one might add, because it is not an island in the proper sense. It is insulated by jungle from the adjoining states of South America, and in terms of cultural and historical experience is very much the last 'island' in the Commonwealth Caribbean chain running down through Trinidad & Tobago and onto Guyana. Guyana became associated with—indeed initiated—the apparent shift to the Left in Caribbean politics when in 1970 the People's National Congress (PNC) government of Forbes Burnham declared the country to be a Cooperative Socialist Republic. The resulting nationalizations and the active pursuit of a Non-Aligned foreign policy maintained the radical pretence for a time; but that image was steadily undermined and ultimately destroyed by the government's resort to coercion and numerous abuses of democracy to preserve its position, together with its manifest failure, in good part as a result of corrupt and inefficient management, to bring about the development of the economy. In retrospect, cooperative socialism can be seen to have been, in the words of the eminent Guyanese political economist, Clive Thomas, merely "an ideological rationalization for the development of state capitalism in Guyana and for the creation of a new class of indigenous capitalist, 'fathered' in the first instance by the state."[14]

In addition to class, race must be fitted into the analysis of Guyanese politics. From the outset, the PNC did not receive much support beyond the African element of Guyana's population, which constitutes only some 38 percent of the total. It first achieved power in 1964, in coalition with a rightwing party, after Britain (with US encouragement) introduced a proportional representation system designed to oust from office the People's Progressive party. The PPP enjoyed the support of the majority Indian sector of the population but was, and still is, led by an avowed Marxist, Cheddi Jagan. After independence was achieved in 1966, Burnham moved to establish PNC-Afro-Guyanese political dominance by widespread rigging of the 1968 election aimed at securing a parliamentary majority for the first time.[15] After 1970, with attention at home and abroad diverted by cooperative socialist rhetoric, the party fully consolidated its predominance. The stages stand out clearly—the stuffing of ballot boxes by the Guyana Defense Force in the 1973 election, the enunciation of the doctrine of the paramountcy of the party in 1975, the fraud of the 1978 referendum on a new constitution, and the terms of that constitution itself which came into effect in 1980 and upgraded Burnham to Executive President with almost dictatorial powers. Add to these events the militarisation of Guyanese society—as over 20 percent of revenue came to be spent on military and police items—and one can well understand the suspicions aroused when in June 1989 Dr. Walter Rodney, a leading radical opponent of the PNC within the Working People's Alliance (WPA), was blown up by a car bomb in Georgetown. As the

Barbadian poet, George Lamming, warned his listeners at the memorial service, "today we meet in a dangerous land at the most dangerous of times."[16]

Although the condemnation of Guyanese abuses of democracy by Commonwealth Caribbean and other governments was never as loud or unequivocal as it ought to have been, the Burnham regime did over time become more isolated regionally and internationally. This had further damaging effects on the already devastated economy and gave rise to the thought that a coup might take place against Burnham by some part of the country's military apparatus when the president unexpectedly died while undergoing a minor operation in August 1985. He was succeeded by Desmond Hoyte (a first vice-president of the PNC under Burnham) who has since sought to revive the economy by rolling back the extensive state sector and reopening links with external sources of finance. Politically, he has not been able to move as fast, although there is evidence that he has wanted to effect a cautious 'de-Burnhamization' of the political system. Some symbolic moves have been made, such as ordering an inquest into Rodney's death and urging greater integrity in public life. Hoyte has also committed the heresy of observing that "the party is not the government."[17] He has worked to maneuver against the Burnham faction in the PNC, which is led by the ex-president's wife, but the truth is that he still does not have control of what has long been a faction-ridden party. His true political intentions cannot be fully tested and it can only be noted that no significant reforms of electoral practice, the key test, have yet emerged.

Through the dark times which Guyana has had to endure since independence, it is remarkable that people of courage have continued to ply the politics of opposition as best they can. Jagan himself, the leaders of the WPA, notably Eusi Kwayana, numerous trade union leaders who have been very active in strike action in the past few years—all have preserved in the political culture the basis of the competitive liberal democratic system which the Guyanese people, alone among Commonwealth Caribbean citizens, have not experienced in the independence era. The last fair election to have taken place in the country was in 1964, a quarter of a century ago in the era of colonialism. However, it does now look as if another free and fair election will take place before the end of 1991, monitored by a number of external observers. The liberalization of the economy, if it is to continue and bring rewards desired by the Hoyte government, will also increase the pressure on the regime to bring the political system rather more into line. Guyana will not spring fully-fledged into liberal democracy, but the time is long overdue for the reintroduction of some genuine competitiveness into its politics.

THE PACIFIC

The military intervention in Fiji in 1987 did to political commentary on the small island states of the South Pacific what the revolution in Grenada did to discussion of Caribbean politics eight years earlier. It gave rise not only to a new interest in the region but also to a line of analysis which emphasized its growing political instability and the threat to a postindependence embrace of liberal democratic norms. Fiji, like Grenada, was seen as the forerunner of other similar political changes. Although nobody matches the hyperbole of the US State Department spokesman who talked of the Caribbean as a 'sea of splashing dominoes' in the aftermath of Grenada in 1979, the 'Fiji effect' was nevertheless born. Attention turned to signs of political unease in Papua New Guinea (PNG) and Vanuatu, the other two leading Commonwealth South Pacific states, and scenarios involving the overthrow of existing regimes were busily assembled. Yet the thrust of much of this analysis has been misleading. It is not that there has been no political tension in both Papua New Guinea and Vanuatu: its existence is undeniable. Nor should it be thought that the South Pacific is free of the danger of instability. It is certainly possible to discern systemic trends at work relating to what used to be called 'modernization'. But the pattern of change is unlikely to replicate that of Fiji. The two coups and the general nature of the crisis of Fijian democracy, has been grasped more in outline than in its complexity. Fiji is an unusual society even in its South Pacific context, and the events there have been more exceptional than normal. They need to be unraveled a little before we can see what are the overall trends.

FIJI

Race is the required starting point. At his first press conference after the May 1987 coup, Colonel Rabuka justified his and the army's intervention as a necessary means of preventing the erosion of Fijian land and other indigenous rights by an 'Indian-dominated' government.[18] This interpretation was subsequently given a wide airing and won for Rabuka a measure of external sympathy, especially in other parts of the South Pacific where he has frequently been portrayed as a defender of indigenous peoples against ambitious immigrant communities living in their midst. It also promoted the view of the Fiji coup as representing the beginnings of a tide of indigenous nationalism preparing to sweep across Melanesia. Yet the figures, when examined, show that only 42 percent of the members of the Fijian parliament elected in April 1987 were Indians. To be sure, 19 of the 28 Coalition members of parliament were Indians: but the new cabinet had been evenly balanced in ethnic terms, certainly by comparison with the fifteen or more years since independence was attained in 1970. The new prime minister, Dr. Timoci Bavadra, was a Fijian and ethnic Fijians had been placed in charge of ministries customarily regarded as prerogatives of the indigenous people, of *taukei*, including Fijian affairs and home affairs, the latter incorporating responsibility for the police and defense force. Indians, on the other hand, had been given portfolios which even under former Alliance party governments had nearly always been occupied by non-Fijians. The one significant exception was foreign affairs. In general, therefore, so far from presaging an Indian grab for power, the composition of the Coalition cabinet had reflected the triumph of multiracialism over communalism. Contrary to popular interpretation, this was the respect in which it challenged some of the traditional tenets of local politics which, for all its apparent openness, had been characterized by ethnic Fijian dominance.

In fact, the Coalition, dismissed by Colonel Rabuka, had been elected because it succeeded in winning a critical 9.6 percent of the ethnic Fijian vote. The causes of this seepage of support away from the Alliance party were varied, but they are critical to an understanding of the brief politics of the Bavadra government. The shift derived partly from a growing commoner assertiveness against chiefly rule, partly from the longstanding disgruntlement of western Fiji against domination by the eastern outer island, and partly from an emergent class consciousness among those living in squatter settlements outside Suva.[19] This last point raises, of course, the issue of the Coalition's alleged 'socialism' and the dominant role played by the Fiji Labor party (FLP) in both the election campaign and the short-lived Bavadra government. Much has been made of the 'leftism' of the new administration, its external connections and its commitment to nonalignment. The facts are substantially less lurid. As a political party, the FLP sat wholly within the well-established Anglo-Australasian social democratic or laborist tradition. It emerged out of the trade union movement and promised sound economic management, rather than any radical reorientation of the structure of economic ownership. Its intended foreign policy was no more than nationalist and Third Worldist in character. It is true that many of the leading lights of the FLP were university graduates at ease in the world of political ideas, but what they represented, above all, was a younger political generation eager to replace the old men of the Alliance whom they saw as wary of change and antagonistic to innovative ideas.

The problem was that these old men had come to believe that the government of Fiji was their natural fiefdom. Led for many years by Ratu Mara, the ruling elite was simply unable to tolerate the existence of the FLP and the Coalition as a government. It threatened a system of patronage and a way of life built up over nearly two decades. The precise connection between Mara, Rabuka, their associates and other members of the Taukei movement has been the subject of much speculation[20] but in the end they did not matter. The social and political circle constituted by the Fijian elite was very small, and it is clear that Rabuka thought he was acting on behalf of the Taukei movement. The Fijian army was less of an independent actor in the making of the coup than is often assumed: it was much more the agent of a deposed elite of frustrated politicians bent upon recapturing power lost at the polls. Whether either the army or Rabuka will remain content with this role is another matter. The second coup in September 1987 reflected a restiveness at being outmaneuvered by the old politicians, but in July 1990 a new constitution was promulgated which gave predominate power to a Fijian Council of Chiefs, a president elected by the Council, a prime minister and a restricted parliament of 37 seats for Fijians (under a franchise weighted against urban voters), 23 seats for Indians and six for other races. The opposition declared that it would boycott the elections, but the army stood guard over these uneasy arrangements and has now almost certainly become a permanent actor on the political scene.

There was nothing inevitable about the two coups. They were not historically predetermined by conflict between Indian and Fijian; nor did they reflect the simple assertion of the primacy of indigenous values over national politics; still less did they represent the reaction of a beleaguered capitalist class confronted by the challenge of socialism. Race and class, as well as generational tensions and provincial disparities, were mixed with patronage and political jealousies in a complex brew of forces which can only fully be understood in the context of a more elaborate survey of Fijian history than space permits here. What does need to be stressed, as with Grenada, is the uniqueness of the mix of factors at work.

PAPUA NEW GUINEA

Papua New Guinea invites comparison with Fiji. According to one widely-articulated line of argument, it too hovers on the brink of a coup which, if it happens, could destroy the functioning system of a democratic government, legitimized by regular elections at national and provincial levels, which has been preserved in the country since independence in 1975. The argument is a combination of the claim that the action of the Fijian army might inspire its PNG counterpart (which cannot be wholly dismissed) and the deeper belief that the Papua New Guinean political system is experiencing many of the same strains which eventually broke Fijian democracy. As we shall see, the possibility of a coup cannot be completely set aside, but it remains unlikely, and it would assuredly not be like Fiji even if it were to happen. The country and its politics are too dissimilar.

The point to stress is that PNG has a different history and culture. It is not so much a state containing two separate nations, like Fiji, as one embracing several diverse ethnic groupings owing allegiance predominantly to loyalty rather than nation. The country's main achievement since independence is to have survived intact and to have forged enough of a national consensus about the means of government to operate (not ineffectively) in the world outside. In these circumstances, it is perhaps understandable that PNG's democratic credentials have to be qualified by reference to a number of longstanding fragilities. A weak party system, shifting factional alignments, frequent floor-crossing by MPs and unstable coalition governments have become the norm, giving an air of endemic instability to political life.[21] The most characteristic symbol of this has been the mechanism of the no-confidence motion which, under the terms of the constitution, allows for changes of government to occur on the floor of parliament and gives incoming administrations only six months grace before they are vulnerable to such challenges. On the negative side, the habit has reduced the effectiveness of government and the consistency and coherence of policy; on the positive side, it has provided a fluidity in politics which has defused tensions. As many have observed, PNG is a country which needs a 'light' governmental presence.

Even within these loose parameters, it has been argued that the political system has displayed a greater degree of stress in the last two years than ever before. Tony Siaguru, a former MP and one of the country's leading political commentators, has talked of the country being 'at the crossroads, and warned that, if 'this slippery, sliding situation' is allowed to continue, then 'there is very little hope for us to pull out of it'.[22] His concern has been echoed by several analysts. The argument in essence is that economic development, prompted of late by a mineral exploration boom, has unleashed new social forces which are beginning to alter the traditional style and conventional rules of political conflict. Evidence is variously drawn from the growing gap between the rich (including many politicians) and the poor, and the consequent emergence of class tensions, the spread of crime and what is called 'rascalism'; most seriously of all, there has been renewed regional dissension containing within it the threat of secession. The latest phase of the long-running Bougainville problem, which blew up in April 1989 and again in May 1990, is the most serious and has led to a level of political violence, including killings, beatings and assassinations hitherto unknown in PNG. Nevertheless, the consensus among analysts still is that PNG is only in a condition of 'precrisis'.

The key to this debate, as everybody appreciates post-Fiji, is the mood of the PNG army. The spectre of a coup has been raised on a number of occasions. In November 1987 when Ted

Diro, the former foreign minister, having been forced to resign for a year or so from government in the face of corruption allegations, publicly observed that conditions were ripe for military intervention, a view rescinded when reinstated in April 1990 as deputy prime minister! Since then, the defense force has been involved in exchanges with the Indonesian army on the Irian Jaya border and suffered losses in repressing the discontent in Bougainville; it rebelled against a cabinet decision to move some of its assets to a new base, rioted briefly in Port Moresby over poor pay and conditions, and been drawn evermore extensively into a general policing role. In other words, it can scarcely be said to be playing the part of a passive political bystander. For all that, the judgment of one of the most informed of the many Australian watchers of PNG, David Hegarty, is worth quoting. While admitting that 'an attempted limited intervention . . . by disgruntled, disaffected, maverick or wild card elements within the army cannot be entirely excluded from a range of considerations', his view is that 'topography, ethnicity, military capability, institutional rivalry and other constraints would seriously inhibit a successful army takeover . . . along the lines, for example, which occurred in Fiji in 1987'.[23] The litany of divergent factors there listed itself enough to make the point that the direction of future political change in PNG, even if it involves the army, will not parallel that in Fiji.

VANUATU

Vanuatu is different again. It experienced a much more trying birth as a state than either Fiji or Papua New Guinea. Ruled jointly by Britain and France as the Condominium of the New Hebrides, it suffered a kind of colonial dualism on top of the linguistic, cultural and regional factionalism which characterizes the South Pacific. French colonial officials openly resisted the advent of independence, which came in 1980, and encouraged a secessionist movement on Espiritu Santo, one of the outer islands, which was only put down with the aid of troops from Papua New Guinea.[24] The country's youthful political leaders, headed by Father Walter Lini, an Anglican priest, weathered the storm and can be said to have gained from the experience. This is, in fact, a factor of considerable importance, for they undoubtedly embarked on the postindependence era with a more robust, assertive and self-confident outlook than the other new leaders of neighboring South Pacific states.

The result has been that, in the intervening years, Vanuatu has gained a reputation for being the most 'radical' of the small states in the region. This commitment to political change is a genuine aspiration of the leadership. The rhetoric of 'Melanesian socialism' has been dismissed by those who point to the fact that Vanuatu also operates a tax haven and a flag of convenience, and the range of viable options facing a copra-exporting state of some 150,000 people is not vast. In foreign policy, however, Vanuatu cut a dash: it actively participated within the Non-Aligned movement, forged agreements with the Soviet Union, Cuba and Libya, bitterly opposed continuing French colonialism and nuclear testing in the South Pacific, and generally shown itself to be reluctant to accept automatically the presumption of Western leadership of the region. What these various stances reflect is not an anti-Western posture *per se*, but a determination to make choices about external relations in accordance with local, rather than alien, priorities.

The Lini government has also shown itself to be a firm supporter of the principles of liberal democracy. His Vanuaaku Pati (VP) has dominated the country's politics since it was founded in the 1970s, but it is opposed in parliament by a coalition of smaller parties, the Union of Moderate parties(UMP). This essentially two-party system reflects, in the man, the historical cleavage between the British and French traditions of the colonial past, the leaders of the VP being schooled by the British and the UNP by the French.[25] The only real threat to the VP's rule occurred in May 1988 when Barak

Sope, the party's secretary-general, attempted to topple Lini and take over as prime minister.

Sope was the man most responsible for the Libyan links which Vanuatu briefly enjoyed and some have seen his bid for power as having ideological origins. This is almost certainly mistaken: it drives instead from simpler considerations, such as ambition and personal rivalry, interwoven, as always in the multi-island states of the South Pacific, with longstanding local loyalties. Lini appears to have successfully seen off the challenge, which further strengthens the political system. As regards comparisons with Fiji or Papua New Guinea, the point is that the small Vanuatu Defense Force adhered to a nonpolitical role in the crisis, giving support faithfully to the elected civilian leaders. The worrying note is that the regime was unquestionably hard pressed at the time of the 1988 protests. Lini was forced to appeal to the Australian government for an emergency airlift of tear gas and might easily have had to request more overt intervention. Such are the nature of the security threats posed to the democratic systems of small, island developing states which do not possess and, for good reasons, do not really want to have an elaborate military infrastructure.

CONCLUSION

General conclusions are not easy to come by. The argument has emphasized the 'exceptionality' of the circumstances surrounding the two most dramatic breakdowns of democratic politics, the Grenadian revolution and the Fijian coup, among the small states of the Caribbean and the Pacific. These events unquestionably cast a shadow over the politics of other neighboring states in the two regions, but Grenada did not set a trend in the Commonwealth Caribbean and, although the lapse of time is less, Fiji seems unlikely to be the forerunner of coups of a similar sort in the South Pacific. As the discussions of Jamaica and Guyana and Papua New

Guinea and Vanuatu make clear, the particular cultures, histories and political situations of each of the 'small island developing states' are sufficiently different to prevent easy generalization. In addition, beyond the cases considered, there are nine other independent territories which fit the category of 'small island developing state' in the Commonwealth Caribbean and seven others in the South Pacific each of which, to varying degree, has some claim to be both parliamentary and democratic.

There are some general observations which can be made. Firstly, it is apparent that the countries of the Commonwealth Caribbean have gone a long way towards the successful elaboration of a liberal democratic order appropriate to the norms and values of the people of the region. This order has come to be characterized by broad fidelity to the Westminster-Whitehall model, fiercely competitive party rivalries, open political discussion and the play of 'big' personalities. In the end, the aberrant cases of Grenada and Guyana reinforce the syndrome because its leading features always seem to have stayed alive in the face of whatever antidemocratic forces have arisen. Contrast, for example, the experience of Haiti. Many reasons may be advanced to explain the emergence and consolidation of such a liberal democratic order in the Commonwealth part of the Caribbean, but they all derive from an appreciation of the colonial past. The denial of liberty represented by slavery put a premium on freedom (of both property and expression) in the Commonwealth Caribbean which has never been overridden and which the Westminster system has certainly proved to be good at preserving. Socialized by over three hundred years of British colonialism, the emergent Commonwealth Caribbean elite could scarcely have become anything else other than liberal democrats. Accordingly, the contemporary reality is that the Westminster system is viewed in the region not as foreign import but as genuinely autochthonous. It has successfully survived the challenges represented by political developments in Grenada between 1974 and 1983 and in Jamaica between 1972 and 1980 and, with luck, will eventually emerge to the grim experience of Guyana. Having been tested in these ways, there is reason to believe that liberal democracy has indeed grounded itself in the political culture of the region.

Secondly, it seems likely that the countries of the South Pacific are, by contrast, just entering a period of political tension which may imperil their democratic inheritance to a greater extent than in the Caribbean. Politics in this region in the postindependence era, although largely adhering (until 1987) to the forms of liberal democracy, have not moved far away from the chief patterns of precolonial times. Those times are, of course, not so distant as in the Commonwealth Caribbean: the Deed of Cession by which Fijian chiefs handed sovereignty of their islands to Britain was only enacted in 1874 and has long been interpreted locally as constituting less a conquest than a temporary period of protection. In short, South Pacific culture, including political culture, survived colonialism in a way that was simply not the case in the Caribbean. Westminster-Whitehall constitutions were therefore grafted onto an existing mode of politics, organized around local rivalries, ethnic tensions and status differences. The conflict of norms represented by the two systems was unproblematic in the 1960s and 1970s when social and economic change was only moving slowly, but became critical in the 1980s when urbanization, labor unrest and middle-class discontent, to list only the most obvious phenomena, began to generate new political tensions. Whether these trends are interpreted as evidence of modernization or the emergence of class conflict, or both, the fact is that the South Pacific mix of traditionalist politics with democratic forms does not seem well-placed to cope with them. Fijian democracy has already gone and that in Papua New Guinea is vulnerable in the medium-term. By contrast, Vanuatu appears to have created a political system better adapted to the management of change. In general, it would appear that liberal democracy must expect to be largely on the defensive in the South Pacific over the next decade.

Thirdly, and lastly, it cannot be claimed that the 'small island developing states' of the Commonwealth Caribbean and the South Pacific are anymore likely to be able to forge and sustain liberal democratic politics as a consequence of their 'smallness' or 'islandness' than are larger or landlocked states. Sutton's initial profile of the political characteristics of small states has stood up well as a mechanism within which to make comparisons. Thus the Commonwealth Caribbean displayed a greater institutional fidelity to the Westminster model than did the South Pacific, although by the standards of other parts of the ex-British Empire both regions were on the faithful side. Governmental pervasiveness was everywhere present, but felt to the sharpest degree by those opposed to Gairy in Grenada, Burnham in Guyana and Rebuke in Fiji. Exaggerated personalism was similarly ubiquitous, seen in both good and bad lights at different times and in different places. A basic political harmony also kept political life within acceptable bounds in most Caribbean and Pacific small states, with the key exceptions being the two with the most marked racial divisions, Guyana and Fiji. As for pragmatic conservatism, the focus on the exceptions (Jamaica under Manley, Grenada under Bishop and Vanuatu under Lini) can be said perhaps to have undermined the general rule. In every case, though, the bearing of these factors on the democratic experience of the Commonwealth Caribbean and the South Pacific was secondary. The states considered here do display a greater attachment to democratic politics than is the norm in the non-Western world, but this does not derive from their 'smallness' or 'islandness'. They are only 'islands of democracy' when viewed from the great sea of Third World authoritarianism.

NOTES.

1. Examples are UNITAR (United Nations Institute for Training and Research), *Small States and Territories: Status and Problems*, New York, 1971, and R.A. Dahl and E.R. Tufte, *Size and Democracy*, Stanford, 1973.
2. Paul Sutton, "Political Aspects" in Colin Clarke and Tony Payne (eds.), *Politics, Security and Development in Small States*, London, 1987, 23.
3. *Ibid.*
4. For a fuller account of this syndrome, see *ibid.*, 8-19.
5. J.C. Caldwell, G.E. Harrison and P. Quiggin, "The Demography of Micro-states," *World Development*, vol. 8, 1980, 953-967.
6. See especially Dahl and Tufte, *Size and Democracy*.
7. For an elaboration of the argument, see Morley Ayearst, *The British West Indies: The Search for Self Government*, London, 1960.
8. A.W. Singham, *The Hero and the Crowd in a Colonial Polity*, New Haven, Connecticut, 1968.
9. See Tony Thorndike, *Grenada: Politics, Economics and Society*, London, 1985.
10. *New Jewel*, vol. 2, no. 11, March 13,1980, 5.
11. The best account of the societal basis of this system is provided by the work of Carl Stone, which is well summarized in his *Democracy and Clientelism in Jamaica*, New Brunswick, 1980.
12. Elaborated in Anthony J. Payne, *Politics in Jamaica*, London, 1988.
13. See Humberto Garcia Muniz, "Defense Policy and Planning in the Caribbean: An Assessment of the Case of Jamaica on its 25th Independence Anniversary," *Caribbean Studies*, vol. 21, no. 1-2, 1988, 67-123.
14. Clive Thomas, "Guyana: The Rise and Fall of 'Co-operative Socialism'" in Anthony Payne and Paul Sutton,

eds., *Dependency under Challenge: The Political Economy of the Commonwealth Caribbean*, Manchester, 1984, 100.

15. The evidence concerning the rigging of the 1968 election is assembled J.E. Greene, *Race vs. Politics in Guyana*, Kingston, 1974,27-33.

16. *Caribbean Contact*, July 1980, 3.

17. *Caribbean Insight*, September 1987, 1.

18. This position is presented in the 'official' account of the coup, Eddie Dean with Stan Ritova, *Rebuke: No Other Way*, Suva, 1988.

19. For a fuller discussion, see Brij V. Lal, *Power and Prejudice: The Making of the Fiji Crisis*, Wellington, 1988.

20. See Robert T. Robertson and Akosita Tamanisau, *Fiji: Shattered Coups*, Leichhardt, New South Wales, 1988, 85-111.

21. See Yaw Saffu, "Aspects of the Emerging Political Culture of Papua New Guinea" in *The Politics of Evolving Cultures in the Pacific Islands*, Hawaii, 1982, 256-279.

22. Tony Siaguru, cited in David Hegarty, *Papua New Guinea: At the Political Crossroads?*, Working Paper No 177, The Strategic and Defence Studies Centre, The Australian National University, Canberra, 1989, 1.

23. Hegarty, *Papua New Guinea*, 12.

24. See John Beasant, *The Santo Rebellion: An Imperial Reckoning*, Honolulu, 1984.

25. See Lamont Lindstrom, *Vanuatu*, United States Information Agency Office of Research Paper, Washington D.C., November 1988.

CHAPTER 3

THE REVIVAL OF DEMOCRACY IN LATIN AMERICA

Paul Cammack

Surveying the record of liberal democracy worldwide up to 1976, Bingham Powell identified a core group of twenty-one countries classed as democratic by five recent studies.[1] Only one, Costa Rica, was in Latin America. Since then transitions from military to civilian rule of one kind or another have taken place in Ecuador (1979), Peru (1980), Bolivia (1982), El Salvador (1982), Honduras (1982), Argentina (1983), Brazil (1985), Uruguay (1985), and Chile (1990). In addition, Venezuela (listed by four of the five studies cited above) has completed thirty unbroken years of democratic rule; Colombia (listed by two) has emerged from the National Front period of controlled succession, and may be considered a democracy in a minimal sense; Nicaragua has seen successive elections in 1984 and 1990 following upon the overthrow of the Somoza dictatorship, the first confirming the Sandinista

Front in power, and the second installing the opposition UNO in their place. Mexico in 1988 experienced its most competitive elections of recent times, and may be judged to be moving reluctantly towards a competitive party system.[2] Paraguay in 1989 saw the bundling of General Stroessner into exile and his replacement, in dubious and hasty elections, by longtime associate and coup leader General Andres Rodriguez, as head of the Colorado party. A democratic revival of major proportions has been underway in the region for a decade, and if only a few of these cases prove to qualify as meaningful democracies and survive, the universe of democratic nations will be substantially extended.

Powell takes as the essential criteria for the identification of a democracy a number of qualities—the legitimacy which rests upon a claim to represent the desires of its citizens; leadership elections at regular intervals in which voters can choose among alternatives; ability of most adults to participate as voters and candidates; secret and uncoerced votes; and basic freedoms of speech, press, assembly and organization. He looks for at least five years continuity, and for actual alternation in power as a result of elections or grounds for a reasonable presumption that a change could be voted for, and would take place if the electorate so decided.

For various reasons, the Central American cases are problematic. The changes that have occurred in the region are not insignificant, but it is unlikely that a consensus could be obtained for the classification of El Salvador, Guatemala or Honduras as democratic regimes in the sense intended by Powell and others.[3] The seven South American cases of transition (Argentina, Bolivia, Brazil, Chile, Ecuador, Peru and Uruguay), along with the "established democracies" of Colombia and Venezuela, provide a much more plausible set, and all but Chile now have at least five years of experience with democracy. The genuinely regional scale of the process of democratization is the first striking feature. The second is that no new democracy has fallen to successful military intervention since the first, Ecuador, was established in 1979; the seven have now totaled fifty years of unbroken civilian rule between them. Thirdly, in every case in which successive elections have been held, oppositions have come to power. This was the case in Ecuador in 1984 and 1988, in Peru in 1985 and 1990, in Bolivia in 1985 and 1989, in Argentina in 1989, and in Uruguay and Brazil (where Collor was an independent) in 1990. The record across the region testifies to the competitive nature of these regimes, if not to their stability. None of the cases of return to democracy over the last decade can be said to represent a safe transition to consolidated democracy. But the evidence above suggests that on the basis of what has been achieved thus far they merit detailed examination. This is particularly clear if we briefly examine the economic context in which these transitions have taken place.

We may begin with some elementary comparative data. Table 1 records per capita GNP figures for the core group of 21 democracies and the eight South American states with five or more years' experience of democracy. With the exceptions of Costa Rica, which lies within the Latin American group, and India, which falls well below it, all the "core democracies" have substantially higher per capita incomes than Latin America. Only Venezuela, with its oil wealth and relatively small population, is within striking distance of the poorest of the "First World" democracies, the Republic of Ireland.[4] After Venezuela, there is a sharp drop to Uruguay; and four of the new Latin American democracies stand below Costa Rica, with dollar per capita income figures of less than one-tenth those of the wealthiest democracies.

These figures give a broad idea of the standing of the new Latin American democracies in comparative terms at the beginning of the past decade, but they may overstate real average differences in purchasing power. Table 2, drawing on the United Nations International Comparison Project, suggests that they do, and provides an alternative assessment

Table 1 **GNP per capita: Core and Latin American Democracies, 1980** (current US$)			
1. Switzerland	15,980	16. New Zealand	6,860
2. Sweden	13,730	17. Italy	6,400
3. Norway	12,830	18. Ireland	4,930
4. West Germany	12,320	19. Israel	4,590
5. Denmark	12,010	20. **Venezuela**	3,910
6. United States	11,590	21. **Uruguay**	2,620
7. France	11,200	22. **Argentina**	2,590
8. Belgium	11,120	23. **Brazil**	2,160
9. Netherlands	11,010	24. **Costa Rica**	1,390
10. Canada	10,180	25. **Colombia**	1,260
11. Australia	10,070	26. **Ecuador**	1,100
12. Finland	9,700	27. **Peru**	1,080
13. Austria	9,360	28. **Bolivia**	570
14. Japan	9,020	29. India	230
15. United Kingdom	8,520		
Source: World Bank, *World Bank Atlas*, 1983.			

of average income levels in 1980. On these figures, the order of the Latin American cases remains unchanged, but they all improve their standing *vis-á-vis* the core democracies, and some variations occur in relative standing between them. While the differences in average purchasing power are not so stark, essentially the same message is conveyed: average income levels are very substantially below those of the established democracies. Tables 1 and 2 together offer us a rudimentary benchmark for the standing of the South American countries at the outset of the "democratization decade."

Table 2 Latin America: ICP Purchasing Power per capita, 1980 (United States=100)			
Argentina	33.5	Ecuador	22.6
Bolivia	14.2	Peru	21.9
Brazil	29.3	Uruguay	37.2
Colombia	24.8	Venezuela	47.4
Source: Reported data from Phase IV of the United Nations International Comparison Project, World Bank, *World Development Report*, 1988, Table A2, p. 270.			

Table 3 tracks changes in per capita GDP per year between 1979 and 1988 for the eight South American countries which experienced transition in the period. It reveals quite substantial differences between the various cases, Colombia standing out as an economic "success story," and Brazil less dramatically affected than the remaining cases. Argentina, Bolivia, Uruguay and Venezuela suffer very sharp declines in per capita income in the first half of the 1980s; Ecuador suffers a sharper setback under the monetarist regime of Febres Cordero after 1986; Peru experiences sharp decline between 1981 and 1983 under the monetarist government of Belaunde, a brief burst of recovery under Alan Garcia, and desperate collapse during the last two years. The general picture, outside Colombia, is clearly one of deep and prolonged crisis, and the prospect of only slow and painful recovery.

Table 3								
Per Capita GNP in the New Latin American Democracies, 1980-1988								
(1980 = 100; bold = transition year)								
	1980	1981	1982	1983	1984	1985	1986	1987	1988
Argentina	100	92	86	**87**	88	82	86	86	86
Bolivia	100	98	**92**	83	81	79	74	74	74
Brazil	100	95	93	89	92	**98**	103	98	96
Colombia	100	103	99	99	100	101	104	108	110
Ecuador	100	101	100	94	95	97	97	89	92
Peru	**100**	101	99	85	86	86	91	95	83
Uruguay	100	101	91	85	83	**83**	89	94	94
Venezuela	100	97	95	87	84	81	83	84	85

Source:
Figures for 1980-1986 calculated from IMF, Financial Statistics; for 1987-1988, GDP figures from Economist Intelligence Unit Country Reports, population increase assumed constant from 1985-1986.

Three significant conclusions may be drawn from these various figures. Firstly, per capita GDP levels are substantially lower than those for the great majority of established democracies. Secondly, the new democracies in South America cover a very wide range, from Bolivia at one extreme to Uruguay and Argentina at the other. Thirdly, in most cases democratization has occurred in a period of seriously declining levels of per capita income, and chronic, prolonged and recurrent economic crisis. Here, though, there are differences, which may be significant, in the relative timing of the moment of transition in relation to the evolution of per capita GNP. In Argentina, the transition came at a low point after a 14 percent drop over two years; following a brief sharp dip in 1985, the low plateau reached under the military has been maintained. In Bolivia, a substantial fall before democratization has given way to a catastrophic decline thereafter and the reaching of a plateau 25 percent below the starting point. In Brazil, the transition came in a phase of rapid recovery but the cycle of rising and falling per capita GDP levels has continued, with a downswing now in force as elections approach. In Ecuador, where transition came early, there was no immediate decline, but the impact of the recession of the early 1980s, followed by the economic collapse under Febres Cordero, adds up to a 10 percent drop since the return to democracy. In Peru, a sharp decline under the first civilian government of the decade, followed by the dramatic collapse that has much more than wiped away the initial recovery under Garcia, threatens to leave GDP levels near to 30 percent lower than they were when the military departed. In Uruguay, sharp declines took place before the transition, as they did in Argentina; in contrast, though, Uruguay has since made and held onto a modest recovery, returning to 1979 levels. The most striking difference is between the two established democracies, Colombia and Venezuela. While Colombia's per capita GDP index has risen by 16 points since 1979, Venezuela's has fallen by 24 points. To complete the picture, it should be noted that Chile made the transition to democracy in a period of sustained positive growth, after a process of change that began in the wake of the catastrophic economic collapse of 1982 when GNP fell back by over 10 percent.

These varied considerations by no means exhaust the range of quantitative data that could be brought to bear on the Latin American democracies. The scattered figures of income distribution, for example, suggest far greater inequality than in any of the core democracies: in Latin America, as much as two-thirds of national income may accrue to the top quintile, in comparison with something around 40-55 percent for the generality of established democracies.[5] Debt-export ratios suggest the depth of the economic crisis and the vulnerability of particular countries (Argentina, Brazil, Peru and Venezuela being the most exposed). Figures on current rates of inflation show Argentina entering hyperinflation,

Brazil and Peru in serious trouble, Ecuador and Venezuela struggling, Colombia keeping control, and Bolivia enjoying stability after hyperinflation in 1985.[6]

Two conclusions may now be drawn from this review of background conditions. The first is that the transitions to democracy currently underway in South America are being made, in general terms, in extremely adverse circumstances. The second, equally significant, is that there are major differences from case to case in terms of performance on different indicators, and the timing of transition in relation to those indicators. Even if one accepts that there might be a straightforward connection between economic circumstances and the prospects for democracy, there can be no presumption that all the new democracies are facing the same circumstances.

Against this background, I wish to address the issue of the prospects for the consolidation of democracy in the light of two contrasting analytical approaches: the tradition of empirical democratic theory which seeks correlations between quantifiable social and economic data and sustained democracy; and historical-structural analysis which focuses more upon social structure and historical process. Finally, in the light of the conclusions drawn, I shall assess the adequacy of the policy recommendations recently offered to rulers of the new democracies by O'Donnell and Schmitter in 1986 and Malloy in 1987.

DEMOCRATIC THEORY AND
NEW LATIN AMERICAN DEMOCRACIES

The Latin American republics have rarely behaved as the proponents of empirical democratic theory would wish. Argentina, the wealthiest and most developed in the early twentieth century, has been the least successful in sustaining democracy: when Menem succeeded Alfonsin in July 1989 it was the first time that a civilian president elected under universal suffrage had been succeeded there by an elected opponent. Chile and Uruguay, next in line on the same criteria, enjoyed decades of virtually unbroken democracy, characterized by high degrees of tolerance and regular alternations in power—although not by universal suffrage in Chile—only to fall to long-term military dictatorship in 1973. Those interventions were part of a series which also affected Brazil and Argentina, thus destroying democracy in a single decade in the most developed states in the region. Bolivia, Ecuador and Peru shared the same fate, while Colombia and Venezuela avoided it. Over the course of two decades the five Central American republics displayed in an even more perplexing array of cases: stable democracy enduring economic crisis in Costa Rica, a personal dictatorship giving way to socialist revolution in Nicaragua, and the imposition or maintenance of military dictatorships elsewhere. Finally, in the current wave of democratization, the poorest countries in the region have led the way. The record thus displays considerable variety between regimes with broadly similar socioeconomic profiles, and numerous outcomes that contradict any linear theories linking socioeconomic advance and the advent of democracy.

Recent reviews of empirical theory give little cause either for confidence in the economic correlations thus far developed, or for the prospect for democracy in Latin America. Assessing the extensive literature on economic preconditions for democracy in 1984, Huntington argued that as countries develop economically they enter a transition zone, but in that zone "what is predictable . . . is not the advent of democracy but rather the demise of previously existing political forms." He concluded that "with a few exceptions, the limits of democratic development in the world may well have been reached." Brazil is his candidate for the regime most likely to become democratic, and he expresses qualified optimism with regard to Chile, Uruguay and Argentina. The latter, however, figures, with Bolivia, Ecuador, Peru, Ghana and Nigeria, in a group of countries where "the alternation of democracy and despotism *is* the political system." Myron Weiner, too, found correlation-based theories unconvincing and makes no forecasts about future democracies, but places heavy emphasis upon former British colonial rule as a shared characteristic of the most successful Third World democracies. Huntington and Weiner both reflect the fact that insofar as empirical democratic theory has focussed on correlation as a means of identifying the possible social and economic preconditions for democracy, the results have been disappointing.

Along with their review of correlation-based approaches, both scholars consider social-structural arguments which relate to the historical emergence and subsequent maintenance of democracy. Huntington, taking his cues variously from the Marxist claim that democracy is "bourgeois democracy, reflecting the interests of that particular social class" and from Moore and Lindblom, asserts that "a market-oriented economy, like a bourgeoisie, is a necessary but not sufficient condition of a democratic political system." As to why this should be so, he offers two reasons: (1) Politically, a market economy requires a dispersion of economic power and, in practice, almost invariably some form of private property. The dispersion of economic power creates alternatives and counters to state power and enables those elites that control economic power to limit state power and to exploit democratic means to make it serve their interests; and (20 economically, a market economy appears more likely to sustain economic growth than a command economy . . . and hence a market economy is more likely to give rise to the economic wealth and the resulting more equitable distribution of income that provides the infrastructure of democracy.[7]

Consistently with this approach, Huntington argues later that democratic institutions "come into existence through negotiations and compromises among political elites calculating their own interests and desires"(p.212); they are more likely to survive if institution-building precedes the expansion of political participation or, in other words, if elites are able first to construct institutions that respond to their own interests, then to channel and control the incorporation of the majority in order to ensure that those institutions continue to serve elite interests. This conservative theory of democracy, familiar from Huntington's other work, is grounded, finally, in a Schumpeterian vision of democracy as a system in which "(the) most powerful collective decision-makers are selected through periodic elections in which candidates freely compete for votes and in which virtually all the adult population is eligible to vote."

Weiner makes similar arguments. He too follows Schumpeter in seeing democracy "as a process of governance and as an institutional framework, not as a government committed to any particular set of social and economic objectives or of a society with particular characteristics." He later quotes Schumpeter's statement that "historically, modern democracy rose along with capitalism, and in casual connection with it."[8] Pursuing the theme, he argues as follows:

> In theory, the link between capitalism and liberal society in which individual rights are respected is that the property-owning middle class needs and supports a regime to pursue its economic interests. Although the presence of such a class does not ensure that democracy will continue, thus far we have not seen a democracy emerge that has not had such a class (p.13).

Turning later to the means by which democratic institutions are to be maintained, Weiner points to the ability of parties in five successful Third World cases(Costa Rica, India, Jamaica, Malaysia and Sri Lanka) to convert themselves into mass-based institutions, and to the emergence of party systems which allow alternation in power:

LIBERAL DEMOCRACY IN NON-WESTERN STATES

> The institutionalization of at least one national party among the electorate and the capacity of one or more opposition parties to win substantial electoral support thus appear to be critical elements in whether a democratic system becomes institutionalized (p.22).

Two simple propositions follow from these two accounts. The first is that representative liberal democracy is the most appropriate political system for market economies (capitalist societies), providing that the two central requirements of responsiveness to the interests of economic elites and regular mass participation through elections if the selection of leaders can be reconciled. The second is that these conditions are best achieved through parties supportive of a market-based economy, able to secure popular support, and capable between them of keeping alternative ruling groups continuously available. These conclusions are in keeping with those of radical democratic theory, which identifies the same set of characteristics but which tends to emphasize the limitations they entail and to deplore the contradictions between such systems and normative values of participation and equality. They are also fully in keeping with the historical record of the development of democratic institutions in the core democracies in which expansion of suffrage has often come as a consequence of inter-elite rivalry, and where the substantive goals of dominant elites have always taken precedence over commitment to democratic procedures.[9] If it is true, as Weiner asserts, that "we have no examples of a democracy that does not have a capitalist economy," it is equally true that we have no examples of capitalist economies in which an elected anticapitalist government has been allowed to survive. The basic message is a simple one: democracy survives when the system meets the needs of the bourgeoisie with the participation of the working class.

As Huntington and Wiener conclude, not every capitalist economy can support a democratic system. In light of the considerations discussed above, the relevant issues revolve less around quantitative correlations abstracted from historical and social context, than around the ability of economic elites in capitalist societies to secure democratic systems which respond to their interests. The presumption would then be that where they fail to do so, some system other than representative liberal democracy will ensue. This suggests in turn that we should pay particular attention to the manner in which such systems were secured in the advanced market economies of today which make up the great majority of the core democracies listed above.

The best starting point for such an enterprise is Lipset and Rokkan's classic essay in 1967 on the origins of European party systems. It was a pioneering historical-structural analysis of party and party system formation. At its core was a focus on the timing, character and effects of successive national and industrial revolutions, and the interactions between them. Lipset and Rokkan traced varied conflicts and alliances arising out of basic confrontations between center and periphery, church and state, agriculture and industry, and workers and employers. They contended that choices in each of the first three conflicts at successive critical historical moments led to different contexts within the class struggles of the industrial era were faced, and to different, enduring systems of political incorporation. Thus

> the crucial differences among the party systems emerged in the early phases of competitive politics, before the final phase of mass mobilization. They reflected basic contrasts in the conditions and sequences of nation-building and in the structure of the economy at the point of takeoff toward sustained growth (p.35).

Lipset and Rokkan argued that the choices made at the crucial historical junctures dominated successively by center-periphery, church-state, and land-industry conflicts explain the variety in party systems, and the different outcomes in each case from the similar impact of class conflicts between owners and workers. They also attached particular importance to the issue of whether mass organizations had been developed by conservatives and liberals before the final thrust to full suffrage took place:

> Where the challenge of the emerging workingclass parties had been met by concerted efforts of counter-mobilization fronts, the leeway for new party formations was particularly small; this was the case whether the threshold of representation was low, as in Scandinavia, or quite high, as in Britain. Correspondingly the "postdemocratic" party systems proved markedly more fragile and open to newcomers in the countries where the privileged strata had relied on their local power resources rather than on nationwide mass organizations in their efforts of mobilization (p.51).

The message is clear where liberal and conservative mobilization had provided modern party organizations before the full extension of the suffrage to the working class (as in Britain and Scandinavia), it proved possible to preserve democratic continuity. Where it had not (as in Italy, France, Spain and Germany) it did not. As we have already seen, elements of this analysis have been taken up elsewhere. However, if individual elements are abstracted out, the full logic of the argument may be lost. Its distinctive feature is that it attempts to move from an initial broad but historically situated focus (upon national and industrial revolutions) to an understanding of particular party systems in Europe as they stood in the 1960s. In its macrostructural historical focus, this approach is quite different in method to that employed by Lipset in his own exercises in ahistorical correlation, and too much of the empirical democratic theory briefly touched on above. It is much closer in style to Barrington Moore's historical essay on the origins of democracy and dictatorship, or to Charles Tilly's historical sociology. Given its focus on varied national combinations and configurations on "common" issues, it implicitly rejects the possibility of meaningful correlations between abstracted socioeconomic indicators and any particular political events; and by its specific focus upon the emergence of party systems (and of enduring democracies) in Western Europe, in specific historical conditions not reproduced elsewhere (the Reformation and the Industrial Revolution), it implicitly argues against any direct reading from the European cases to other times and places. In other words, it invites scholars of other regions to consider what a similar exercise might suggest, rather than to draw hasty conclusions based upon simple parallels and contrasts. In the following section, I consider how the record of party politics and democracy in Latin America might be approached in the same style.

CLEAVAGE STRUCTURES AND PARTY SYSTEMS IN LATIN AMERICA

From the point of view of comparative historical sociology, the "national" and "industrial" revolutions which Lipset and Rokkan take as their starting point may be seen as European expressions of two genuinely global processes, one of the emergence of a system of nation-states, the other of the coming into being of a global capitalist economy. Both processes have a history in which the European experience has been central, but one in which it has been part of a greater whole. A first step towards an approach to Latin America in comparative framework derived from the Lipset-Rokkan exercise would be to identify the distinctive forms which these "national" and "industrial" revolutions took in the region, and to assess the consequences by looking for key conflicts which might have played the shaping roles which Lipset and Rokkan attribute to successive core-periphery, church-state, land-industry and owner-worker conflicts in Europe. The first task is to identify the specific form of the national and industrial revolutions or, more precisely, the character in Latin America of the emergence of nation-states, and the spread of the international capitalist economy. It will then be necessary to identify conflicts constitutive of key cleavage structures, and the various patterns which emerged from country to country within the region. This is too large a research project for a comprehensive account to be given here, but some broad outlines can be suggested as a point of departure.

On the two dimensions identified, Latin America has a distinctive regional history. Practically all the Latin American nations, formerly colonies of the Catholic Spain or Portugal, came to independence in a brief period between 1810 and 1830 in large part as a consequence of the impact upon Spain and Portugal of the Napoleonic Wars in Europe. They, therefore, share a common history of *early political independence*. Secondly, they were all drawn into the emerging global capitalist economy in a role that complemented the industrial revolution already gathering strength in Europe, but which at the same time reflected the different circumstances prevailing in Latin America's distant, sparsely populated and relatively undeveloped new states. Without exception, the Latin American states were drawn into the Europe-centered world economy as suppliers of raw materials and importers of manufactured goods. The process was most dynamic in the half-century between 1880 and 1930, in many instances after serious instability had marked the immediate period after independence when different factions struggled for control. They thus experienced a process of internal economic change which was complimentary to the industrial revolution in Europe but which, in their case, was based upon *export-led development*.

For Latin America, then, the relevant parallels to national and industrial revolution, from the perspective of comparative historical sociology, are early independence from Iberian rule and an export-led development from the late nineteenth century on. On this basis, three very broad contrasts can be drawn with the European experience. Firstly, the process of state formation arose from a single source, the breakdown of Iberian rule. Within this process, the major contrast came between the survival of Portuguese-speaking Brazil as a single entity, and the breakup of the large Spanish viceroyalties into a number of independent states. Even so, within two decades the map of the region took on a shape that would be readily recognizable today. The following period was marked by sometimes intense hostility within and between states, but Latin America did not become a focus of struggle *between* major powers. Secondly, while major disputes often centered around church-state conflict, the Catholic church never experienced a challenge from the Protestant offshoots of the Reformation. Thus while conflicts were sometimes acute and long-lasting, and gave rise (as in Columbia) to significant party expression, they were never as complex in Europe. On the whole, where they were prominent, they tended to provide a basis for a single cleavage between conservatives and liberals, reinforcing a parallel cleavage between social and economic groupings either based on the colonial structures, or challenging them in the name of free enterprise and free trade. They played a part in the major changes which preceded the commitment of the region to export orientation, but rarely persisted into the twentieth century. Thirdly, and most significantly, the battle between land and industry that structured so much political exchange in Europe was never properly joined in Latin America. Until 1930, manufacturing industry took second place to export production, either mineral or agricultural. The consequence was the reinforcing of the dominance of landed elites, either directly or in concert with the mostly foreign exploiters of mineral resources.

On each of these points, variations from country to country led to patterns of conflict and alliance as different between each other as those depicted by Lipset and Rokkan for Europe. They were differences within a common framework provided by the common experience of Iberian rule, Catholic dominance, early independence and export orientation. For our limited purposes, the key to subsequent developments is provided by the common consequences of all these various developments for the fourth Lipset-Rokkan variable, conflicts between workers and owners and the consequences in terms of political incorporation. Put briefly, *few opportunities or incentives existed before 1930 for the construction of mass organizations into which the working class might be incorporated.* The primary cause here was the dominance of export-oriented development. Landowners and mineowners, seeking to keep the costs of production as low as possible, had no incentive to extend citizenship to their workers; the workers themselves were often divided by distance, status, and category (from peasant producers to migrant workers drawn by debt); industry was too weak to figure, or to wish to figure, as an ally of labor. As to the conflicts that arose on regional bases, or between liberals and conservatives, where they were not resolved through the raising of temporary armies, they generally gave rise to exactly those clientelist structures, or at most urban political machines, whose fragility in Europe Lipset and Rokkan underline.

The consequence of this was that, prior to 1930, even where the franchise was most extensive, the working class had not been substantially incorporated into mass organizations devised or controlled by elements of the bourgeoisie. In Argentina, where the franchise had gone furthest, the working class (clustered in Buenos Aires) was for the most part either excluded by lack of citizenship or loyal to the Socialist party. The Radicals had clashed with workers after the World War I, and relied upon a political machine based upon the white-collar government employees and the middle classes of the capital. In Uruguay, the farsighted welfarism of Batlle had a similar base. In Brazil, the question of labor had been notoriously defined by the last president of the Old Republic

(1889-1930) as a "question for the police." In Peru, the dictator Leguia (1919-1930) had made an initial attempt to bring the working class into a populist alliance but the attempt broke down in 1922, leading to the emergence and banning of APRA and the Socialist party which directed their efforts to workers in the export sectors and the urban economy respectively. In Columbia, Ecuador, Bolivia and Venezuela, urban industry was in its infancy, and export workers were either scattered and differentiated (as in Colombia), or isolated, few in number and subject to close control, as elsewhere.

The consequences of the failure to incorporate workers and peasants into mass organizations were dramatically exposed by the crash of 1920 and the ensuing depression. This had a political influence across South America which went far beyond its immediate economic impact, which was sometimes relatively mild and short-lived. The depth and lasting consequences of its political impact, in contrast, stemmed precisely from the limited extent of political development at the time. Coming in the wake of growing social challenges to existing regimes since the World War I, the crash and the depression spelled the end of export-led development as a growth strategy around which consensus could be built by the elites that had come to the fore over the previous fifty years. The existing elites lost not only their consensus on the "rules of the game," where they had achieved it, but their ability to organize support from their electorates. New counterelites pushed to the fore, either within existing parties or outside them, and the result was the breakdown or slow death of existing party systems in every case.

In Argentina, in a classic demonstration of a major Lipset-Rokkan hypothesis, Peron tapped an unworked area of the "support market," after more than a decade of authoritarian rule following the immediate military coup of 1930, winning an unchallenged majority among the formerly immigrant and new migrant working class. The resulting dynamic led eventually to the bloody and destructive alternation of the military and the Peronists in power. In Bolivia, after two decades of political turmoil following the disastrous Chaco War, successive attempts by military caudillos to launch counterelite regimes and a conservative reaction leading to the government of Urriolagoitia, the urban middle class opposition—MNR—linked up with the radicalized tin miners to put together the initially radical coalition that made the Bolivian Revolution of 1952. In Colombia, strong dissident factions arose in the Liberal party, espousing first agrarian reform and then urban populism under the dynamic leadership of Gaitain. The strength of these currents split the party and provoked antidemocratic currents resulting in the failure of consensus, the exacerbation of local rivalries, and the breakdown of political and civil society during the period of *la violencia*. In Ecuador, the excluded urban masses rallied behind the episodic populism of Velasco Ibarra which was never strong enough, either to impose itself politically for the longer term, or to provide the social base for the kinds of economic program pursued with greater effect in Argentina and Brazil. In Peru, a brief experiment with military populism canceled out the rival populism of APRA; control reverted to conservative elites only to give way successively to experimental regimes seeking an alternative way forward before the long-term military intervention and right-wing populism of General Odria, and the military-backed but ineffective reformism of Belaunde. In Uruguay, the Blanco and Colorado parties tried to keep their system going, after a very brief flurry of military interest in the 1930s, by reinforcing and extending the clientelist range of their parties, until they lost touch with the social roots, and collapsed into military authoritarianism in the 1970s. And in Venezuela, after the long Gomez dictatorship, *Accion Democratica* emerged after a decade as a radical challenger, only to be swiftly ousted by a broad conservative reaction. Again, military rule was the outcome.

The exogenous shock of the depression rendered existing ruling elites incapable of either resolving their own differences amicably, or winning popular support for their programs. In circumstances in which neither the peasantry, where it existed, nor the working class had been brought into politics, it proved impossible after 1930 to combine responsiveness to the needs of the dominant classes with the rallying of sufficient popular support to make democracy work. In the best cases, either traditional political forces were able to hang on, despite increasing incapacity to act effectively on behalf of the interests of economic elites (as in Colombia, Peru and Uruguay), or populism took over as a "second-best" solution, based on a precarious alliance which continually threatened to tilt the balance too far towards the economic interests of workers, stifling in the meantime local sources of political opposition and potential alternates in power as in Argentina (for less than a decade), in Brazil, or in a different way, in Bolivia under the MNR. In Ecuador, the lack of party development and the persistence of a weak and contradictory populism led to repeated exchanges between populism and military rule. In Venezuela, the three years of democracy between 1945 and 1948—themselves ushered in by a reformist military intervention—were all the democracy the country had to show since Bolivar, over a hundred years earlier, had likened the challenge of postrevolutionary government to that of ploughing the sea.

Through all these episodes, each country retained the particularity of a political dynamic whose outlines had been traced during the period of export-led development. But, for a generation, the shared failure prior to 1930 to incorporate national majorities into mass-based political parties imposed a similar dynamic on each country, giving rise to a political cycle which began with the loss of political capacity on the part of the elites in power at the time of the crash and ending in an episode of protracted military rule.

One final "world event" created a further critical historical juncture in this cycle. Just as, according to Lipset and Rokkan, the Bolshevik Revolution had a decisive effect upon the shaping of worker loyalties after 1917, so the Cuban Revolution of 1958-1959 had a decisive effect on the character and organization of military rule in the final sequence of the cycle. Before 1958 (In Colombia and Venezuela) the military leaders who came to the fore eventually essayed forms of Peronist populism. In the wake of the Cuban revolution they backed reform in those countries where national majorities still awaited incorporation (in Ecuador and Peru), or reaction where they faced a mobilized working class (in Argentina, Brazil, and Uruguay). In Bolivia, where the revolution had come and gone by the mid-1960s, an attempt was made briefly at a genuinely popular mass-based regime under Torre and Ovando, before Banzer stepped in with a repressive regime akin to those of the Southern Cone.

Lipset and Rokkan found for Europe that "the 'center-periphery', the state-church, and the land-industry cleavages generated national developments in *divergent* directions, while the owner-worker cleavage tended to bring the party systems *closer to each other* in their basic structure" (1967, p.35). The same reading can be made of the history of party systems in Latin America. After 1930, each country follows a similar cycle of instability leading eventually to protracted military rule, and in each case the root cause is the same: the failure to incorporate national majorities into the political system before the crash of 1930 undermined the already weakened efficacy of the different systems that had arisen during the period dominated by export-led growth. We may now consider the implication for stable democracy in the future.

THE PROSPECTS FOR DEMOCRACY

Two basic propositions may be advanced with regard to the issues of transition to democracy and consolidation in the new democracies. First, the termination of long-term military rule in failure has created a "window of opportunity" for civilian elites to install political regimes which could perform the double task of satisfying the needs of the bourgeoisie and gaining the support of national majorities. Second, however, the requirement for a successful transition, and those for a successful consolidation of democracy, may be diametrically opposed. Whereas it can be argued that a successful transition requires the creation and maintenance of a national consensus, including a decision to shelve, for the moment, issues of social and economic reform and a respect for military prerogatives and power, consolidation cannot be expected—in the historical and current circumstances of Latin America—without decisive movement on each of these fronts: a movement from grand "centrist" coalitions to genuine alternatives put forward by separate organized parties, a willingness to tackle pressing social and economic reforms, and a capacity to define the constitutional role to the armed forces in a manner consistent with clear civilian authority over the use of military power.

The window of opportunity opened to civilian elites arises from the fact that, by the end of the period of military rule, both economic elites and national majorities were thoroughly disaffected. The latter consequence is not remarkable, particularly in the repressive Southern Cone regimes which laid civil and human rights waste about them. But the former is of equal significance, although not so frequently remarked. The middle classes who reached out to the military for salvation found, to differing degrees from case to case, that they had unleashed a monster. In Argentina, the military created the worst economic crisis the country had known, and launched the self-destructive invasion of the Malvinas in an effort to turn to a popular nationalist tradition for support, thus admitting their final defeat at the hands of Peronism. In Uruguay and Brazil, they found the economic elites increasingly restive at their exclusion from policy-making as the economic situation deteriorated in the early 1980s.[10] In Bolivia,

Banzer's dreams of oil-driven wealth dwindled in the late 1970s. Elsewhere, the populist or reformist policies pursued were never to the taste of leading economic interests. Long-term military rule settled an issue that had not been settled in previous briefer periods of intervention: it showed that the soldiers were no better able to govern for the longer term than civilians had been. Particularly in the more recent Southern Cone cases, arbitrary military rule did something that years of civilian rule had signally failed to do. It restored national faith in liberal democracy. Finally, the record of guerilla activity and leftist insurgency, mixed as it was, that had brought the military to power in the post-Cuban years, tempered the desire on the left for genuine social and economic reform with a degree of moderation which gave significant leeway to the moderate or conservative leaders who came to power in the wake of military withdrawal.

However, if these circumstances provided an opportunity for civilian elites committed to capitalist development to enjoy significant levels of popular support without immediately committing themselves to sweeping reform, this was a benefit of the transition rather than a permanent condition. It was the failure of elites to provide channels for popular participation and the satisfaction of popular demands which had launched the cycle that led to civilian rule. None of the parties coming to power had a tradition or a record on this score upon which they could rest. It was therefore inevitable, particularly in the circumstances of deep economic crisis, that a serious intent to respond to the needs of national majorities would be required before long, and that alternatives would be sought out if it were not eventually forthcoming.

In the light of these considerations, some of the advice recently offered to the leaders of the new democracies seems singularly inappropriate, as it focuses entirely on the circumstances of the transition to the exclusion of any evaluation of the realism of the proposals put forward, or of the likely demands of the process of consolidation. I examine two lengthy statements in detail: the first from James Malloy in 1987, the second from Guillermo O'Donnell and Philippe Schmitter a year earlier.

MALLOY ON THE TRANSITION: "LEARN TO LIVE WITH IT"

In his recent discussion of the period of transition, Malloy takes it as axiomatic that in Latin America "there is no unilinear tendency toward democracy or toward authoritarian rule. Rather, the predominant pattern is cyclical, with alternating democratic and authoritarian 'moments'." The danger is, then, that unless avoiding action is taken, the present moment will Prove to be simply one more turn of the wheel, democracy giving way in due course to dictatorship once more. In the past, he argues, the "concrete behavior of critical civilian leaders," along with their inability to solve key issues of public policy, had led to failure. There is, however, "a key voluntary dimension to the process." The actions of individuals can make a difference.

On just how individual leaders should seek to turn that voluntary dimension to account for the survival of democracy, Malloy is brutally clear. In the absence of convincing general theories of Latin American political development

> The best we can come up with is an approach that allows us to produce rationally plausible explanations of past dynamics that hold for as many cases as possible and to project from them a set of ongoing constraining situations and "prudential" rules of action that will indicate certain trends (pp. 237-38).

In this prudent spirit, Malloy offers a number of specific proposals. The search for definitive solutions to economic and political problems should be abandoned in favor of "a series of *salidas* or short-term resolutions of specific problems"; the direction of these should be "to contain the movement toward compression and decompression of power within a single outward juridical form rather than oscillation between outward forms by means of coups d'état"; This will produce "hybrid regimes which assure democratic political participation and maintain civil liberties, while giving the executive quasi-authoritarian power in times of crisis." For this to happen, constitutional engineering will be required in two areas: the electoral process will have to be meaningfully related to governance by means of legislative coalitions that can underpin strong executive power, while political parties mediate between socioeconomic groups and the executive apparatus of the state. In addition, "military and civilian leaders will have to compromise and form *de facto* coalitions so that the military find it in their own interest to back a strong civilian regime in moments of crisis" (pp. 256-57).

Malloy believes that cyclical shifts between authoritarian and democratic rule are generated by underlying forces which have not gone away. The best practical response is to contain those shifts within a single flexible regime, and to hope to muddle through successive crises as they arise. Although he rules out broad general models and theories, he still feels able to advocate a single set of rules for all occasions. He offers no hint of how one should seek short-term resolutions to such pressing issues as the debt crisis, and savage falls in levels of income among the poor. He makes no distinction either between the politics of transition and the politics of consolidation, and indeed his approach makes the distinction inappropriate. Moreover, his prudential rules, which center on the idea that civilian leaders must simply adapt themselves to the enduring features of an immutable underlying reality, derive directly from his initial assumption—taken as axiomatic—that the cycle of democratic and authoritarian rule is an eternal one. He makes no attempt to explore the historical roots and trajectory of the cycle of political instability in the region since 1930. The idea that Latin America is unavoidable subject to equally powerful democratic and authoritarian impulses, hitherto expressed in cycles of democratic and authoritarian rule, virtually determines in advance the advice he offers: learn to live with it.

O'DONNELL AND SCHMITTER ON THE TRANSITION: "HOPE AGAINST HOPE"

A second set of prudential rules for action, linked to a broader analysis, can be found in O'Donnell's introduction to the second volume of *Transitions to Authoritarian Rule* and in the extended essay by O'Donnell and Schmitter which constitutes the fourth and final volume of the set. O'Donnell, like Malloy, finds many of the fundamentals that led to the breakdown of democracy unchanged, but argues that one major and positive transformation has taken place. The armed forces still play a central role, democracy still has shallow and ambivalent roots, levels of social and economic inequality continue to be high, and there is no sign of significant economic or political pacts underpinning the present democracies. However, one thing has changed for the better. In the wake of the negative experience of protracted authoritarian rule, "most political and cultural forces of any weight now attach high intrinsic value to the achievement and consolidation of political democracy." In the circumstances, he argues that there is scope for "purposive human action" that would improve the prospects for democratic consolidation. In his joint essay with Schmitter, O'Donnell spells out a policy agenda derived from this analysis. In its general outlines, the advice offered is as stark as that offered by Malloy. First of all, "the property rights of the bourgeoisie are inviolable"; second, "to the extent that the armed forces serve as the prime protector of the rights and privileges covered by the first restriction, their institutional existence, assets, and hierarchy cannot be eliminated or even seriously threatened." In the circumstances, "the only realistic alternative for the Left seems to be to accept the above restrictions and to hope that somehow in the future more attractive opportunities will open up." These emphases recur throughout the text, and lead to a number of specific recommendations close in spirit to those offered by Malloy. Social and economic reforms must be ruled out during the transition period. The military must be given a creditable and honorable national role, allowed to develop a spirit of corporate professionalism and given the appropriate resources. Employer associations and trade unions "must help each other to acquire a reciprocal capacity for governing the behavior of their respective members." The wave of popular mobilization which is to be expected must be tamed through elections, and parties must "show themselves to be not only, or not so much, agents of mobilization as instruments of social and political control." And parties of the Right-Center and Right must be "helped" to do well, and parties of the Left-Center and Left should not win by an overwhelming majority.

The case for concentration on the establishment of political democracy and for the exclusion of any social or economic content is defended on two grounds: The first relates to the value of political democracy in itself and the degree to which it is compatible with radical social and economic change. The second relates to the prospects for incremental reform in the future. On the first point, O'Donnell and Schmitter argue that "the instauration and eventual consolidation of political democracy constitutes *per se* a desirable goal." They add that a simultaneous attempt to secure improved levels of social justice and economic equality may provoke renewed intervention. More controversially, they suggest that the pursuit of greater social and economic democracy would require "the installation of a popular authoritarian regime which is unlikely to respect either the guarantees of liberalization or the procedures of political democracy." On the second point, they argue that "increment-ally and consensually processed change," compatible with "the values embodied in liberalization and political democracy," is possible in the future, and likely to have more enduring effects than premature attempts at radical change. They envisage, in this respect, "a sequence of piecemeal reforms, in response to a wide range of political pressures and policy calculation."

There are fundamental similarities between these recommendations and those put forward by Malloy. O'Donnell and Schmitter, too, propose a single set of rules for all occasions; they offer no concrete solutions to current problems, let alone for future eventualities; and they propose careful piecemeal initiatives, with substantial reforms postponed indefinitely into the future. Finally, a single assumption—that the pursuit of economic and social reform would destroy the already fragile prospects for democracy—governs the conclusions reached. We are not offered any immediate prospect of significant improvement; instead, we are enjoined to place our faith in possibilism or more, bluntly, to hope against hope.

CONCLUSION

At first sight, the advice offered by Malloy, O'Donnell and Schmitter is hardheaded and realistic. But in the light of current democratic theory as reviewed above, and the past history of party politics in Latin America, it has a central flaw. It simply refuses to face up to the central problem of representative democracy in market economies: the need for elites to devise forms of political organization which satisfy their interests while permitting national majorities to choose their leaders through the electoral process. In other words, it overlooks the fact that if elites offer nothing substantive, other political entrepreneurs are bound to capture significant shares of the market. The challenge is particularly daunting in Latin America, in view of the accumulated social debt, the expectations arising from the ending of military rule, and the depth of the current economic crisis across the region. What is more, Latin American elites in the new democracies have shown little will in the past to moderate their defense of their inherited privileges sufficiently to accommodate any possible compromise.

LIBERAL DEMOCRACY IN NON-WESTERN STATES

It was natural, and perhaps necessary for successful transition, that civilian politicians should come together in a broad alliance committed to securing military withdrawal. But Malloy, O'Donnell and Schmitter fail entirely to tackle fundamental issues raised by the need to build viable parties in the wake of transition. There have been promising signs in this area, particularly with regard to the breaking of deadlocks that seemed to rule out any prospect in the past of alternation in power. The organization of Christian democratic and social democratic currents in Ecuador, the coming to power of APRA as a governing party for the first time in Peru, the emergence of alternatives to the MNR in Bolivia, the restoration of the Radicals in Argentina, and the rise of the PMDB in Brazil all seemed to promise change in the basic structure of competitive party politics. Only in Uruguay was the anachronistic multiple-list system and resulting factionalism carried over unchanged into the period of new democracy. The extent to which party organization has matured has varied widely however. Where it has made least progress, it has been because leaders have sought to build alliances around themselves rather than through parties.

Secondly, when emphasis upon the need for consensus and cooperation between parties has led to attempts by opposition leaders to echo centrist governing parties—as by Cafiero for the Peronists in Argentina—party and national electorates have chosen clear alternatives which seem to represent interests and perspectives neglected by the narrowing of choice entailed in the search for the middle ground. Successful democratic politics comes from the engineering of clear alternatives within broad limits laid down by the need to reproduce the market economy over time. Given the history and present circumstances of Latin America, such alternatives will not emerge without some conflict, and some risk to stability, in the short-term. The task may be a difficult one, and the chance of success slim, but Malloy,

O'Donnell and Schmitter are in danger or surrendering, at the outset, to the inevitability of eventual failure.

Similar considerations apply to the issues of social and economic reform. If some move is not made in the direction of recognizing that elites in Latin America enjoy enormous privileges in terms of national and international comparisons, and that there are pressing injustices which it is in the long-term interests of the elites themselves to have resolved, popular protest is to be expected. The urban unrest that has proliferated recently in Brazil, Argentina and Venezuela may be no more than a portent of what is to come; and the skillful arguments deployed by Malloy, O'Donnell and Schmitter in favor of self-restraint are unlikely to carry great conviction among the numerous urban poor of the region.

Finally, to argue that the military are potential coup-makers and must therefore be left untouched is to offer a counsel of despair. Between the preservation of military privileges as they stand, and a revanchist onslaught on military institutions, there lies a vast distance. Between the two there is room, and an urgent need, for a systematic implementation of institutional changes to subordinate the military to constitutional civilian control. Stepan provides a convincing account of what is needed, and why: the contrast with the hands-off approach advocated by Malloy, O'Donnell and Schmitter could not be more telling.

It is remarkable, in many ways, that the new democracies in Latin America have survived as long as they have. It may be, though, that the blinds are swiftly coming down on the window of opportunity opened by the failure of long-term military rule. The analysis argued in this chapter suggests that a focus on the immediate circumstances of the transition which disregards the longer-run historical context is likely to misinterpret the current situation. Additionally, it suggests that these various cases are best approached in a historical-structural framework of the kind touched on by Huntington and Whiner, and provided for Europe by Lipset and Rokkan, which seeks to trace the specific class requirements for functioning democracy and to relate them to patterns of incorporation of national majorities into party systems.

NOTES

1. J. Bingham, Powell, *Contemporary Democracies: Participation, Stability and Violence*, Harvard U.P. Cambridge, 1982. The other four studies were Rustow, Banks Dahl, and Butler, Penniman, and Ranney. The 21 cases are Australia, Austria, Belgium, Canada, Costa Rica, Denmark, Finland, France, West Germany, India, Ireland, Israel, Italy, Japan, the Netherlands, New Zealand, Norway, Sweden, Switzerland, the United Kingdom, and the United States.
2. For an assessment, see Cammack, 'The Brazilianization of Mexico', *Government and Opposition*, vol. 23.3, 304.20.
3. The changes that have taken place in Central America are significant, as they represent the breakdown of alliances between the military and the oligarchy as a basis for regimes in the region. The policy of "democratization" is a defensive move prompted by the success of the Sandinista revolution in Nicaragua. Even so, there is as yet no basis for accepting El Salvador, Guatemala or Honduras as democracies. For a contemporary account which supports this conclusion, see Booth and Seligson.
4. It should be noted, though, that the same source gives per capita GNP figures for Spain, Greece, and Portugal of US$5,230, US$4,160, and US$2,300 respectively. Portugal would figure among the Latin American cases if non-Latin American additions to the core list of democracies were considered.
5. The data are scattered, and rarely recent. See Sheahan (1987), ch. 2 for a discussion. Powell (1982, Table 3.5, p.48) shows a range from 39% for Australia to 54% for France, for sixteen of the core democracies, with Uruguay at 48%, Costa Rica at 60%, and Venezuela at 65%.

6. The orders of magnitude are staggering: Bolivia and Colombia, 15-30%; Ecuador and Venezuela, c. 100%; Brazil and Peru, c. 1,000%; Argentina, c. 10,000%.
7. Huntington, 1994, 204-205.
8. Whiner, 1987, 12. The citation is from Schumpeter, 1975, 296.
9. The clearest of many examples is the exclusion from the franchise of blacks and poor whites in the period of reconstruction in the United States after the Civil War, as a means to achieving the "Prussian" alliance of northern industrialists and southern landowners. See Bensel, 1984, 73-88.
10. Stepan (1985) provides consistent evidence on this point.

REFERENCES

Banks, A. (1971). *Cross-Polity Time Series Data*, MIT Press, Cambridge.

Booth, John, and Mitchell Seligson, eds. (1989). *Elections and Democracy in Central America*, University of North Carolina Press, Chapel Hill.

Bensel, R. (1984). *Sectionalism and American Political Development. 1880-1980*, University of Wisconsin Press, Madison.

Butler, D., H. Penniman, and A. Ranney, eds. (1981). *Democracy at the Polls: A Comparative Study of National Elections*, American Enterprise Institute, Washington.

Dahl, R. (1971). *Polyarchy: Participation and Opposition*, Yale University Press, New Haven.

Huntington, S. (1984), "Will More Countries Become Democratic?" *Political Science Quarterly*, 99, 2, 193-218.

Lipset, S. and S. Rokkan (1967), "Cleavage Structures, Party Systems, and Voter Alignments: An Introduction," in S. Lipset and S. Rokkan, ed., *Party Systems and Voter Alignments: Cross-National Perspectives*, Free Press, Glencoe, 1-67.

Malloy, J. (1987). "The Politics of Transition in Latin America," in J. Malloy and M. Seligson, eds., *Authoritarians and*

Democrats: Regime Transition in Latin America, University of Pittsburgh Press, Pittsburgh, 235-58.

O'Donnell, G. (1986). "Introduction to the Latin American Cases," in G. O'Donnell, P. Schmitter and L. Whitehead, eds, *Transitions from Authoritarian Rule: Prospects for Democracy,* 4 vols., Johns Hopkins University Press, Baltimore and London, 1986, vol. 2, 3-18.

Rustow, D. (1967). *A World of Nations: Problems of Political Modernization,* Brookings Institution, Washington.

Sheahan, J. (1987). *Patterns of Development in Latin America,* Princeton University Press, Princeton.

Stepan, A. (1985). "State Power and the Strength of Civil Society in the Southern Cone of Latin America," in P. Evans et al., eds., *Bringing the State Back In,* Cambridge University Press, New York.

Stepan, A. (1988). *Rethinking Military Politics: Brazil and the Southern Cone,* Princeton University Press, Princeton.

Weiner, M. (1987). "Empirical Democratic Theory," in M. Whiner and E. Ozbudun, eds., *Competitive Elections in Developing Countries,* American Enterprise Institute, Washington, 3-34.

CHAPTER 4

LIBERAL DEMOCRACY IN SUB-SAHARAN AFRICA

Keith Panter-Brick

One must begin with a word of caution. Any account of democracy in Africa faces two fundamental difficulties—both are problems of perspective: one of time, the other of space.

Democracy is measured over time; it is not acquired overnight. It is secure only insofar as it is institutionalized and tested. The history of the African states, as presently constituted, is still very short. They are, with few exceptions, colonial creations, their frontiers the arbitrary imposition of European powers. Neither precolonial nor colonial antecedents can be said to have laid firm foundations for democracy in the post-colonial state. Traditional practices, however well they may have survived, are too localized and varied for nationwide purposes. Colonialism, for its part, offered little experience of democracy. The colonial administration was not accountable to those it governed. African participation was restricted to local councils, to traditional leaders or those rising to prominence through education. Some Africans were recruited as colonial administrators. Some Francophone Africans did enjoy French citizenship and a few even became parliamentarians or ministers in Paris. Only late in the day did power come to be more widely shared, and once independence was in sight, African voters were more concerned with staking out a claim to a share in the promised land than with holding a government to account. Only the post-independence period can provide satisfactory evidence of institutionalized democracy and that period is all too short to see it in proper perspective.

The second difficulty is simply one of number, of the immensity of the continent and its plurality of states, and of knowing how far each African state requires separate consideration. In what respects are they susceptible to general analysis and overall classification? Most academic studies have looked at tropical Africa from a single perspective, colonialism being seen in many respects as a unifying experience, producing in the postcolonial period a common set of problems and a limited range of possibilities. Thus, the limits and the prospects for liberal democracy are much the same for all African states. However, as John Dunn has warned us, the perspective of causal explanation is retrospective, that of political appraisal is forward-looking. However contrary to democracy the past may have been, there might be grounds for entertaining the possibility of a more democratic future. The discovery whether such grounds exist or not requires an examination not only of the general situation in which African states find themselves but of each state's particular circumstances.

ANALYSIS OF A GENERAL NATURE

Academic analysis has not stood still over the last thirty years, nor has everyone seen African government and politics in the same light. Interpretation has gone through several phases, one conceptual framework after another finding favor for a time. In a sense, there has been a circular movement. The most recent writings, like those of the early 1960s, allow for a certain dynamic variability within the political system. Analysis of a tentative and open-ended nature allows for a range of possibilities, including an element of democracy. The kind of analysis which found favor in the intervening years left no room whatsoever for liberal democracy.

Most early analysis took the view that African governments were responding to a set of functional imperatives. They were said to be committed to achieving national integration through a process of modernization. One-party government was accepted, at least hypothetically, as instrumental to the purpose and a sympathetic ear was sometimes lent to the ideology of one-party rule, namely, that it was circumstantially progressive, even democratic, although structurally precluding the competitive politics of Western-style democracy. The focus of academic study was the party in power, in particular the different types of response to functional demands, as revealed by different styles in leadership and corresponding strategies of both national integration and social change.

In the 1960s Coleman and Rosberg identified two prevailing tendencies or patterns, one of which they called 'pragmatic-pluralistic' and the other 'revolutionary-centralizing'. They took into account not only the party's structure but its ideology and the kinds of relationship which it sought to establish with interest groups, individual citizens, its own members and state institutions.

By the late 1960s and early 1970s, Africanists had to try and find explanations for a very different set of circumstances:

military intervention, a much more obvious display of authoritarianism, factional conflict and economic stagnation. Theories of Third World dependence and of capitalist underdevelopment lay to hand. Africa was nothing more and nothing less than a peripheral appendage of a worldwide capitalist system which had been responsible for colonization in the first place and which had never withdrawn. Governments may have been Africanized but not the control of economic policy. A governing elite has prospered in a parasitic fashion, but not the general body of citizens. On this view, politics was nothing more than intraclass factionalism, a competition for the spoils derived from this neocolonialist system. There were, however, exceptions. Some revolutionary-minded nationalist movements, having managed to seize power and free their countries from dependency upon Western capitalism, had established or were in the process of establishing a system of 'democratic socialism'.

Another school of thought interpreted the change as having been self-engendered. The role of government had extended, administration had expanded and the public purse emptied, largely to private advantage. Governments having laid their hands on virtually all the major sources of wealth—external trade, the currency, foreign investment, outside aid—and these having become the basis of private estate rather than the public domain—competition for participation in government and access to spoils was intensified. Leading positions in government, in administration, in parastatals were closed off for the benefit of those already in place. In the process, the political system was fundamentally transformed. Elections, if still held, offered no effective choice. Compliance was secured through the offer and acceptance of patronage and the selective incorporation into an all-pervasive system of spoils.

Moreover, control of the government having become such a prize, no holds were barred in struggling to win or retain possession. All means to this end became legitimate. Inevitably, the military were the best placed to seize control; but their rule was scarcely any different. Indeed, it proved in many cases even more arbitrary and corrupt. The postcolonial state had thus blossomed, not however into liberal or socialist democracy, but into a highly unstable form of patrimonialism or personal rule.

This Weberian concept of patrimonialism was just as antithetical to liberal democracy as were neo-Marxist concepts of dependency and underdevelopment. So also was the concept of personal rule. In the early 1980s, Jackson and Rosberg's classification ranged from at worst tyranny to at best the rule of someone who, like a prince, is inclined to share power but always retains the capacity to withdraw it as he pleases. In any case, the system was one in which there were no restraints upon the ruler other than those which pertain to him personally; that is to say, his own capacity to secure compliance—no institutionalized constraints, no rules, no procedures that he cannot disregard if it appears expedient to do so.

Later years have brought further revision and a less constrictive conception of the opportunities for some form of liberal democracy. It is now questioned whether previous analysis had not exaggerated the place of the state in African society. The postcolonial state, endowed with the territorial boundaries staked out by the colonial powers, has inherited a population skilled—it is said—by colonialism in the tactics of coexistence. The postcolonial state may claim greater authority and to be less alien, but given the plural nature of society, its ethnic and cultural diversities, and the predominant subsistence economy, the state has been unable to impose its authority on its own terms. This incapacity derives not only from its imperfections, which might perhaps be remedied, but from the ability of those who formally come within its jurisdiction to impose their own limits. To a varying degree, they choose whether or not, and to what extent, they are incorporated as citizens beholden to a central government. There is a 'precarious balance' (the title of a recent book edited by Rothchild and Chazan) between the power of the state and the resistance of society. The state can attempt to regulate, to direct, to tax, and to distribute benefits in furtherance of its own aims. Society, however, either as individuals or as groups, has a degree of autonomy in how to respond. The state is more firmly established externally through recognition by the international community of states than it is internally in the eyes of its own nationals. Even when there is an apparent hegemony of control, the reality is that of an uneasy coexistence.

Such a description is the broadest of generalizations and highly abstract. It needs to be filled out by some account of society itself, of the various (often fluctuating) group identities to which individuals subscribe at the different levels at which they make their presence felt, and of how collective standpoints come to be expressed. The most common identities are ethnic but these are by no means fixed and invariable. A great deal of bargaining goes on at levels, not only between group spokespersons and state officials, but also to the exclusion of government, and in ways which negate official policy. The role of those in official positions is often ambiguous, a factional rather than a public interest predominating. Nor is everybody dependent upon official largess to the same extent. It has been argued that peasant populations have resources of land and labor, enabling them to fend off a state control which they find more vexatious than beneficial. Goran Hyden certainly found the Tanzanian peasantry to be 'uncaptured' by the state.

The implications of this mode of analysis are far-reaching. The state is neither master of nor servant to a body of citizens in any well-regulated fashion. There is little or no habitual or confident reliance upon the state, either for the enforcement of rules or even for personal security. The public domain, however extensive it purports to be, becomes only one of the arenas to which individuals and groups might turn for the satisfaction of their needs. Africa has long been familiar with nomadic peoples who, recalcitrant to authority and boundaries when these impose unacceptable restriction, shift ground. Likewise, have learnt to disengage from officialdom, whenever it is convenient or calculated to be advantageous to do so. There is an option, well known to all members of organizations who find that their views are not carrying any weight, namely, to choose an exit. It is not necessary to emigrate. There are alternatives. Many producers and traders, for example, have developed their own informal economy, operating markets outside state control, and turning to smuggling in defiance of the state.

Might this precarious balance mature into an uneasy state of equilibrium? Might an authoritarian government seeking compliance from a multifarious society, under little inescapable obligation to conform, settle for some form of coexistence? This is an assumption underlying various recent classifications. At the end of the 1980s, Rothchild distinguished two types of interaction: 'hegemonial-exchange' and 'bureaucratic-centralist,' a dichotomy very similar to that formulated by Coleman and Rosberg in relation to political parties in the early 1960s. Chazan *et al.* give a more elaborate sixfold classification. One category, 'pluralist,' is used to denote those few states where one finds 'a mixture of bargaining, compromise, and reciprocity', 'a notion of the separation of powers', 'fairly vibrant representative structures', and some 'interest-group involvement', combined with 'a strong elitist strain'. Again one is reminded of much earlier classifications, namely those of Edward Shils. Was not one of his categories 'tutelary democracy'?

THREE CASE STUDIES

An examination of particular cases has to be historical for reasons already stated. Democracy takes time to become institutionalized. Where there is a record of political instability, there will be breakdown and regression. Constitutional reforms designed to establish or reestablish democracy will be short-lived, and progress will be at best intermittent, halting, incremental, and observable only over time.

African states are still very much in the process of formation. It is perhaps a permanent condition for all states but those of sub-Saharan Africa are inchoate, still clay in the hands of those who shape the rules and practices of the political system in accordance with their own predilections and vested interests. The contest for hegemony in domestic African politics is akin to that in international politics. There are similarities in the ways a certain overall authority is asserted. Because of the plural nature of society, some recognition has to be accorded to separate identities. There may be a tacit acknowledgement that different regions and different communities within the country should share power at the center because none happens to occupy a dominant position. Power might be more or less equally shared, and an agreed set of rules for governing the country brought into operation. Examples of a shared compromise may not be easy to find—a forced inequality may be much more likely—but the state being weak in relation to society, there will be practical limits to any exercise of hegemonic power. It may in fact prove very short-lived if it is abused, or if it is dependent upon alliances which prove unreliable.

Three case studies, of Nigeria, Senegal and Botswana, will illustrate the diversity of sub-Saharan Africa and the specific nature of each country's problems.

NIGERIA

Nigeria is unique in Africa, in being a federation. The balance of power with which Nigeria was endowed at the time of independence—three Regions, one the equal of the other two combined—was a bone of contention from the start. Politics, both nationally and regionally, was dominated by regionally-focused parties, seeking to consolidate their power regionally and to exclude their rivals from power nationally.

Little was left of democratic tolerance and impartial administration by the time of the 1964 federal elections and especially the 1965 elections in the Western Region. A coup, carried out ruthlessly by a mutinous section of the army in January 1966, brought the military to power. It merely deepened mistrust and set in motion a series of events which culminated in civil war. A clumsy attempt to enhance central authority, on the part of one set of military leaders, prompted a counter-coup. When a swing in the opposite direction threatened the breakup of Nigeria, a solution was imposed by force of arms. As a result, 12 States replaced the Regions and central authority emerged much the stronger.

Government has been, ever since, in the hands of the military—or rather an alliance of military, police and civilian administrators—except for a brief interlude, 1979-1983. The military, discredited by remaining in power long after the end of the civil war to no good purpose, had prudently given way to elected politicians. They proved no better, and the military had little difficulty in resuming in 1983 where it had left off in 1979.

The character of government has varied very little over the years, be the government elected or self-appointed. Oil has provided an abundance of revenue for governments, and control of the spending, invariably in ways which bring personal enrichment, are the only questions which really matter. There is intense competition for a share of the cake. Military governments may have eased some of the tension by increasing periodically the number of states (now numbering 30) and by ensuring that local authorities (now numbering over 500) receive a share. The spoils of office have thereby been decanted but the character of politics remains the same.

This is not to say that no distinction is to be made between military and civilian rule. The Nigerian military, which rules by decree, claims supreme authority in all matters. This claim has been contested by the judiciary, which during the 1970-83 interregnum had earned considerable respect for upholding individual rights and freedom of the press. But it fought a losing battle after 1983, for the military simply ruled that the validity of its decrees could not be questioned in any court of law. As was said by the Court of Appeal in 1985, on an application for a writ of habeas corpus, "the courts of law must of now blow muted trumpets." The Nigerian judiciary awaits a further turn of the wheel, the return of an elected government which cannot declare itself above the law, as do many other Nigerian citizens, with growing impatience.

The military has taken its time in preparing a return to barracks, in a manner not very convincing, for it has more than once put a spoke in the wheels. Successive military governments have in fact led the politicians a merry dance, by controlling in considerable detail the party political process and by repeatedly finding fault. The end of military rule, the sole purpose of the politicians' patient submission to all the procedures and pronouncements emanating from the military government and the National Electoral Commission, has thus proved elusive. Much time has been lost—and money spent—all to no avail.

It was decided to limit the number of parties to two and to bar from party leadership not merely all persons convicted of corrupt practices but all those responsible for government, past and present, be they civilian, police or military. More than a dozen potential parties were formed ostensibly by a "new breed" of politicians, all jostling for official recognition. Assessed by the National Electoral Commission in accordance with prescribed desiderata, e.g. substantial and well distributed membership, internal accountability and an electoral manifesto which matched the country's needs, all were found wanting. They were accused by the Commission of presenting fictitious membership rolls, of being faction ridden and of only partially disclosing their source of finance.

This opened the way for the military government to draw up its own version of the two-party system. One party was given the name Social Democratic Party (SDP), the other was called the National Republican Convention (NRC). Each was provided with a manifesto, one designed to be left of center, the other right of center, the center being a copy of the military's own conception of national good. The government also prescribed procedures for the enrollment of members, the choice of leaders, local, state and national, and the nominatim of candidates. It provided the two parties with offices, equipment and adequate working capital. The choice of leaders was to be based on "personal merit"

The politicians spent 1990-1993 conforming to this scenario, stage by stage. Local authorities were the first to be elected at the d of 1990, and in these elections the government experimented with a system of voting which it claimed to be simpler and more reliable, namely that of lining up behind the portrait of one or other candidate. It was not a success. Only 25% of the registered electorate was prepared to be identified publicly with one side or the other, roughly matching the number who had been enrolled as party members. Moreover, those turning out to vote had to stand in line most of the day. Manifestly unpopular, the system was abandoned. In the subsequent elections, of state governors, state assemblies and a bicameral federal parliament, turnout improved. The results were encouraging to both parties—the SDP was ahead in the national elections but the NRC won several states—and the military government declared itself satisfied.

There remained the final and crucial stage, the elections of president and vice-president, on a joint ticket. The two parties had still to nominate their candidates, in national conventions to which delegates had been duly elected. At this point the military government called a halt, expressing its dissatisfaction with the politicking of the party delegates, who were apparently more concerned with producing a balanced ethnic and religious ticket than with personal merit. The military thus remained in overall command, flanked by elected representatives, a strange dyarchy but supposedly only a temporary one, pending a rerun of the nominating process.

Caretaker committees were appointed to replace party executives and all those who had earlier stood for nomination were disqualified. Frustrated, the politicians had little option but to concur, but again to no avail. Although a presidential election was finally held, in June 1993, the result has never been officially declared. An Association for Better Nigeria, which had tried but failed to have the election postponed, managed while the count was still incomplete but the SDP allegedly in the lead, to obtain a court order precluding the Electoral Commission from proceeding any further. A rival association, the Campaign for Democracy thereupon sought the assistance of the courts in demanding publication of the results. The SDP candidate, M.K.O. Abiola, and his teammate, Batanga Kingibe, allegedly won 19 of the 30 states. However, the military government took upon itself the responsibility of declaring the annulment of the election.

More than a year later, a military government is still in place, unwilling to concede Abiola's claim to be president, yet unable to force his supporters into accepting an alternative. General Babangida, having failed to persuade the SDP to take part in fresh elections, without Abiola as its candidate, or to join the NRC in an interim coalition, was himself persuaded in August 1993 to step down in favor of a civilian led administration. New dates were set for presidential elections but General Abacha, Minister of Defence in the civilian-led administration, jumped the gun and declared himself head of state in November 1993. He installed his own Provisional Ruling Council and abolished the elected legislatures which had existed in limbo for more than a year.

This ambiguous reassertion of military authority, and the arrest of Abiola on charges of treason, after he had defiantly declared himself the lawful president of Nigeria, has brought matters to a head. The hope that the military might possibly voluntarily return to barracks has largely evaporated. Abiola is by no means everybody's first choice but the time may have come to force the issue, a matter of principle being at stake.

Many trade unionists and workers having come out to strike in support, a state of widespread civil disobedience prevails. The British and American governments have added their pressure, as has the Secretary-General of the Commonwealth. The outcome is uncertain and some face-saving compromise remains a possibility.

SENEGAL

The Senegalese political system has been an amalgam of three different spheres, each originating in colonial rule. One is the consequence of political freedoms granted in the nineteenth century to Africans born and resident in four coastal towns. They had all the rights of French citizens and, although by the 1920s they still numbered only a little over 20,000, their influence, at least in municipal politics, was undeniable. Their political heirs, that is the better educated more sophisticated members so the Senegalese electorate, are today's party activists, accustomed not only to debating political issues but also to having a hand in the determination of public policy and its administration.

This political elite has little in common with another part of the electorate—the majority—which is incorporated into one or other of the Muslim Brotherhoods (murridiyya, tijaniyya, qudiriyya). Mostly peasants engaged in the cultivation of a cash crop—peanuts—they have little or no control over their own material welfare. Their spiritual leaders, the marabouts, provide the land and direct the marketing. In any case, their faith inclines them to defer in all matters, the marabouts being attributed with powers to hold misfortune at bay and to offer protection from evil. As in colonial days, the authority of the government is mediated by that of the marabouts, whose cooperation is indispensable.

The people of the Casamance region constitute the third sphere. It is an area of the country which has long defied central authority. A separatist movement is nurtured not only by geographical isolation, but also by ethnic and religious differentiation. This southern part of Senegal is separated from the north by The Gambia. It is more convenient and profitable to trade, clandestinely, with Gambians than via Senegalese officialdom. Moreover, while some Casamance people are Muslim, others have been converted to Catholicism and many remain pagan. It is not an easy milieu for any party to control and several attempts to enforce central authority have been met by armed resistance.

By the time of independence, in 1960, a pattern of political interaction had emerged. Whenever the urban elite is politically divided, as is normally the case, marabout support can be decisive to the outcome. In the 1950s, Lamine Gueye, who had the backing of the French socialist party and most of the urbanized electorate, nonetheless lost out to Leopold Senghor, whose vigorous defence of African culture swung the marabouts to his assistance. Again, in 1962, when President Senghor and Prime Minister Mamadoo Dia fell out, it was Senghor who prevailed. Mamadoo Dia's populist ideology and radical program for social and economic change was seen as a threat to the status of the marabouts and of their business interests. In siding with the President, they deprived the Prime Minister of essential parliamentary support. When he attempted to defy a vote of censure, and called for military support, he was arrested and sentenced to life imprisonment.

Over the next few years, Senegal conformed to the general trend observable in most newly independent African states. It became a one-party state. However, the Union Progressiste Senegalais (UPS) preferred patient use of the carrot to brutal use of the stick. A revision of the electoral law virtually assured it a monopoly of seats in the National Assembly. Any party seeking parliamentary representation was required to nominate a complete list of candidates, who stood collectively, not individually. Small parties, enjoying only localized or dispersed support, found it difficult to compete. Many opposition groups, offered places on the UPS's own list and one or two ministerial appointments, were progressively undermined. The more obdurate were prevented by repressive legislation from opposing the government in any organized fashion. In the 1968 elections, the UPS list was returned unopposed. It was a de facto monopoly, never proclaimed de jure. Even if freedom of political association was curtailed, a variety of opinions continued to be expressed in private.

The UPS claimed to be a 'unified' party but, having absorbed rather than repressed opposition, it was the home of factional leaders, competing for place, parliamentary nominations, official appointments and other spoils of office. The demise of opposition might have been prolonged, had the government been efficient, had the principal source of revenue not been peanuts, a crop badly affected by drought, had the price of oil not rocketed, had the country's dependence on foreign aid not been chronic and had essential outside assistance not been conditional, to some extent, on Senghor remaining faithful to his professed belief in pluralism. In the circumstances, it was deemed prudent to relax the restrictions. Tentatively, at first, in 1974, when approval was given to the formation of Abdoulaye Wade's Parti Democratique Senegalais (PDS), more systematically in 1978, when the party system was given an ideological classification. The electorate was to be presented with a fourfold choice, between a conservative, a liberal democratic, a social democratic and a Marxist-Leninist party. Senghor's own party appropriated the socialist label and left its rivals to accommodate themselves as best they could to the other designations, or to resort to a boycott of elections. In the 1978 elections, when the turnout was 63%, the Parti Socialist (PS, ex-UPS) won 82% and the PDS 18% of the seats in the National Assembly. The obligatory ideological labels were probably irrelevant to the result. More at issue were the relative advantages of staying with the party in power or supporting an opposition party which had some hope of securing representation. Only the PDS, virtually indistinguishable ideologically from the PS, offered that hope.

However that may be, Abdou Diouf, who became President of Senegal in 1981 when Senghor chose to return from office, saw no advantage in continuing to exclude or to harness rival parties. Some regulations still apply, e.g. there can be no use of religious denominations, but otherwise parties are free to participate in elections and to identify themselves as best they please. Nonetheless the government still stands accused of obstructing the opposition. In successive elections, held at 5-yearly intervals, official results show PDS candidates steadily gaining support but never sufficient to win control of the government. In presidential elections, Diouf won 83% of the vote in 1983, 73% in 1988 and 58% in 1993. Wade's share progressed correspondingly from 14% in 1983 to nearly 26% in 1988 and 32% in 1993. The parliamentary results were similar. The PS, which won 111 of the 120 seats in 1983, dropped to 103 in 1988 and 84 in 1993. Moreover, turnout declined to 58% in 1983 to less than 50% in 1988, and in the 1993 parliamentary elections, it was less than 40%.

Opposition parties, the PDS most vehemently, protested with some justification that these figures misrepresent public opinion. The 1988 results were greeted with riots, leading to Wade's arrest. Various allegations of electoral malpractice have been made: a selective distribution of the cards which entitle one to vote; voters denied the right to vote in secret; inadequate provision for an impartial count of ballot papers. The opposition's slogan "supi"—meaning change—echoed a widespread demand. Many must, however, have doubted whether a change from a government led by Diouf to a government led by Wade would make mush difference. Indeed, PDS opposition had been put into abeyance for a period of eighteen months in 1991-92 when Wade and three other PDS leaders accepted ministerial office. Who gained thereby is questionable. It gave the PDS leaders a vantage point from which they prepared the forthcoming election but it left opposition supporters disoriented and increasingly apathetic.

The conduct of the 1993 elections turned out to be as controversial as those of 1988 despite, this time, the presence of international observers. All-party agreement to improved procedures had promised free and fair elections but two of the improvements had unfortunate consequences. The first allowed a dispensation of normal registration procedures. Those who shortly before polling day had come of voting age, had changed residence or had been discharged from the armed forces (in Senegal, they do not have the right to vote) could apply to a magistrate for a special permit which entitled them to vote. This proved a loophole. It is not known how many voted in this manner. No more than 38,000 was the government's claim. At least ten times that number was the opposition's allegation. The first figure refers to the number officially issued, the second to the blank or counterfeit forms filled in fraudulently and used to inflate a party's score.

The other improvement to backfire was the composition of the electoral commission. It was headed by a senior member of the judiciary but all the other members were party representatives. Their disagreements produced a deadlock. The commission relied upon figures sent in from thirty-one centers and especially the comments made thereon by election officials and party observers. These were in many cases contradictory, inconclusive and difficult to assess. The commission was faced with a formidable task and, given its composition, an impossible one. In the course of deliberations on the results of the presidential election, the representatives of opposition parties were uncompromising. They demanded either that the election be annulled or that a second ballot be held, as required when no candidate achieves an absolute majority. In the end it was left to the Constitutional Council to declare Diouf reelected. It was not a very convincing outcome. Not only had the judge in charge of the electoral commission been unable to arrive at any conclusion: the president of the Constitutional Council had dissociated himself from the proceedings by resigning. He had chaired the committee which had prepared the new electoral law and his resignation was a recognition of its failure to bring about an improvement in the conduct of elections. One change was made for the parliamentary elections held two months later. The commission was obliged to declare the results within five days of the poll. But the presidency had been the vital contest and the parliamentary elections were an anticlimax, marked by an even greater rate of abstentions—nearly 60%. The opposition gained seats but not enough to upset the PS's majority.

The PS thus remains the dominant party, open to challenge but continually in office, either alone or leading a coalition. However, little of no progress has been made in reshaping the economy, reducing the country's dependence on foreign aid or improving the living standards of ordinary people. The task might be made easier if a PS-PDS coalition were to be formed, as in 1991-1992. The foreign governments and banks who are Senegal's lifeline are said to urge this. But it has been twice deferred by acts of violence, for which the government has sought to hold the PDS responsible. The first occurred immediately after the results of the presidential election had been announced. Babacar Saye, vice-president of the Constitutional Council, was assassinated. The second followed a 50% devaluation of the currency in January 1994. In a riot, five policemen were killed. An opposition meeting, held on the day of the riots, had broken up in disorder, with calls to take to the streets. PDS leaders were questioned and some of them detained, notwithstanding parliamentary immunity. On the second occasion Wade himself was detained. He and others were released only in July and thereafter acquitted.

The rift between the PS and the PDS is part of a more general worsening of the political situation. The mutual support than has linked the party in power and senior marabouts is less in evidence and less decisive. Neither the one nor the other has much influence over the growing number of youths living in the towns. The established authorities have little to offer them, neither employment, nor proper housing nor inspiration. The lowering of the voting age to 18 in 1993 brought more of them into the political system but they are more likely to participate in street protests than to support the government. Some are enrolled in a fundamentalist Islamic movement, the MWM. This has been banned and its leader imprisoned. As for so long in Casamance, so now in the towns, PS rule appears more repressive than democratic.

BOTSWANA

In Botswana, as in Senegal, one party, the Botswana Democratic Party (BDP), took an early and decisive lead in elections and has remained in power ever since. Opposition parties have however been free to contest elections and there has been remarkable little complaint that failure at the polls is due to electoral malpractice. There has been in fact no need for it, let alone temptation. The opposition parties have been patient enough to wait for better days.

In the first—and only—election prior to independence, the opposition was wrong-footed on a vital issue, Botswana's relations with South Africa. The BDP was unwilling to expose the country to an out and out confrontation with South Africa on the issue of apartheid. Botswana was economically linked to South Africa—by a customs unions, a common currency and lines of communication. Moreover, had Botswana allowed itself to become a threat to South Africa, there would almost certainly have been military retaliation. The other two parties contesting the 1965 election, the Botswana People's Party (BPP) and the Botswana Independence Party (BIP) were much more bellicose. They reflected the views of men who, while in South Africa as migrant workers, had been active in the African National Congress and the Pan-African Congress. When the South African government clamped down on these two organizations in 1961, they returned to Botswana from where they hoped to continue the struggle. Ready apparently to put Botswana in the front line irrespective of the consequences, they were easily dismissed by the BDP as hotheads.

The BDP also had the good fortune to be led, until his death in 1980, by Sir Seretse Khama who embodied both traditional and modern values. His father having ruled over the Bamangwato, he had the status and all the prestige accorded in Tswana society to hereditary chiefs. His people, the most numerous of the Tswana kingdoms, elect no fewer of one third of the seats in parliament. At the same time, Sir Seretse had been educated abroad, had assimilated modern ideas and had even married an English girl. He had thereby aroused the antipathy of white South Africans, been declared by British authorities not to be a "fit person" to succeed his father, and accordingly exiled. He became a "cause celebre." His own people, after initial reservations about his marriage, gave him their support. The British administration, one it became engaged in decolonization, gave more weight to African than to Afrikaner opinion, and so sought his cooperation. His own personal saga had made him a national figure. His was the only name known throughout Botswana. He suited the conservatives, worried lest more radical minds take over. As a reformer, fully committed to the principal of elected authority, he was also acceptable to the tiny but influential and indispensable middle class. His partner in organizing the BNP was Quett Masire, a commoner and journalist, one of the leading "new men." It was a formidable combination, which no opposition party was able to match.

The opposition parties, having lost so decisively the 1965 election, sought both to unite between themselves and to attract support from traditional rulers, but they had little success on either count. The Botswana National Front (BNF) which was to have united the opposition became instead a third, albeit the leading, opposition party, alongside the BPP and the BIP, even contesting some of the same seats as the BPP. Only two traditional rulers gave the opposition any support. In one case, it was soon withdrawn. In the other, it backfired. Bathoen II, chief of the Bawaketse had fallen out with the government, so much so that he resigned the chieftaincy in order to contest the 1969 election and become the BNF's presidential nominee. His intervention had a striking effect locally but less so nationally. In the three Nawaketse seats contested, the BDP's vote was cut by as much as two-thirds, down from 95%-96% to 29%-40%. One of the defeated BDP candidates was the Vice-President, Quett Masire, against whom Bathoen had chosen to stand. The wider and longer-term effect of Bathoen's flirtation with the BNF was not so beneficial. It was a cause of dispute between more moderate and more radical elements within the party, who eventually went their separate ways. The opposition parties have, in fact, thrived best among non-Tswana minorities. The Kalanga electorate, strong in and around Francistown, constitute one opposition stronghold. The Bayei, Bakhalaghadi and Basarwa peoples in the West constitute another. The capital, Gaberone, with its very mixed population, is a third.

These areas provide the opposition parties with a handful of parliamentary seats (never more than 7) and an occasional majority of elected seats on district councils.

Thus from the outset, the BDP managed to occupy the high ground on the two crucial issues, links with South Africa and links with traditional Tswana authority. It went on to consolidate this commanding position in the same firm pragmatic fashion.

First, it left government policy very much to an expatriate bureaucracy. The colonial civil servants were encouraged to stay on, if only because there were too few qualified Tswana to take their place. They continued, as in pre-independence days, to initiate policy as well as implement it. Ministers were content to exercise a watching brief.

Secondly, the BDP government encouraged foreign investment, especially in the mining of minerals. To a chorus of opposition objections that the country was no more than a neo-colonialist state, subservient to foreign and in particular

South African interests, the economy expanded, and the governing party continued to ride high. Botswana became the world's third largest producer of diamonds, its per capita GNP has been one of the highest on the African continent, and the government has extracted a considerable rent from the mining companies.

Thirdly, this income was not squandered in conspicuous consumption. It was, admittedly, used to build up activities of interest to chiefs and politicians, notably cattle ranching. But the lot of the ordinary herdsman and his family was also improved by governmental inputs into the rural areas. Water was made more accessible, schools, roads and health centers were built. During the long periods of drought people had not been left to starve and die. The rural poor, by custom deferential, have been not so much alienated by the new wealth as comforted by what came their way, and by the opportunities for advancement, which education and patronage have provided.

The hegemony and cohesion of the BDP has not weakened noticeably over the past 25 years. At the death of Seretse Khama in 1980, Vice-President Quett Masire took over, the highest office thus passing without incident from a Mongwato to a Monwaketse. Quett Masire's authority was confirmed in the 1984 elections. The party's vote was an overall 78%, the highest since 1965, and it was only slightly lower than usual in the Bangwato constituencies, averaging 85%.

The opposition is still disunited but the BNF has begun to emerge as much the strongest. It won 20% of the vote in 1984 and increased this to 27% in 1989, when it contested every constituency except one. The opposition remains, however, concentrated in minority areas and in the towns, where inequalities in housing conditions and spending power are more blatant, especially relative to the expatriate community, and therefore more resented.

It is the rural areas which remain difficult terrain for opposition parties. The great distances and the scattered population—half live in small settlements of less than 500—make campaigning an expensive and time-consuming business. The kgotla, an assembly of the adult male—but not female—population, provides a forum for the discussion and criticism of government policy and its administration, but by custom party disputes are not allowed. If explicitly party views are to be expressed, a party has to call its own assembly, called a "freedom square." These are more easily convened in urban than in rural areas. There are few more economical alternative means of reaching the electorate. There is press freedom but little commercial incentive to publish or circulate newspapers. The paper with the largest circulation (30,000) is a government publication, issued free. A BNF weekly has a circulation of only 5,000. The radio is government controlled and gives little coverage to party politics, except at election times. There are few organized groups, apart from trade unions, teachers' associations and churches, to be harnessed for party purposes.

The government, obliged to contend in recent years with better organized and more telling opposition, has continued to enjoy overwhelming support. The 1994 elections, due in October, might bring some change. Constituency changes to take account of urbanization give six more seats to the towns and these are likely to be won by opposition candidates. Some cases of corruption within government have come to light, leading to the dismissal of ministers and factional conflicts within the party organization. All this could weaken the BDP and strengthen the opposition, but whether it will be sufficient to put the Botswana political system to the crucial test—a reversal of the BDP's parliamentary majority—is doubtful.

A GENERAL REVIEW

These three case studies illustrate the difficulties of commenting in general terms on politics in Sub-Saharan Africa. They do, however, indicate some of the obstacles which have stood in the way of those striving to make government more responsible, more accountable, more liberal Colonization, contrary to declared purposes, gave authoritarianism a headstart. True, it conferred constitutional rights, subsequently curtailed, but these had scarcely time to become properly established before being easily negated in the name of national unity. Botswana was an exception to the more usual development of the one party state and military government, as illustrated by Senegal and Nigeria.

The reforms of the 1980s usually fell far short of those conceded in Senegal. Almost invariably, the ban on opposition parties remained in force, tempered by some form of primary elections. In some cases, these provided no more than an internal contest for the right to be acclaimed unopposed as the people's duly elected representative. In other cases, several party nominees were presented to the electorate which made the final choice. Primaries of this latter kind were however applied only to parliamentary and never to presidential elections. At best, as in Zambia, there was the possibility for voters to say "no" and not just "yes" to the sole presidential candidate. These limited reforms merely worked to the benefit of the president, the one person who was irremovable. It scarcely enhanced the power of the ordinary citizen. Limited to either abstention or a restricted voice in the reshuffle of parliamentarians, the electorate had no effective institutionalized means of influencing the conduct of affairs.

In the 1990s, African governments have come under pressure, both internal and external, to abandon altogether the one party system. The collapse of communist party hegemony in the USSR and Eastern Europe left them ideologically isolated, although pleas that liberal democracy is not appropriate to Africa can still be heard. The easing of East-West rivalries also threatened them with economic and financial isolation. Nearly all African governments are in grave financial difficulty. Some have even depended upon foreign aid to pay the salaries of their employees. Outside support cannot be suspended overnight, western capital being already so deeply involved, but the conditions for its continuation can be, and have been, altered. African governments are now expected to liberalize their economies and their political systems.

The response to this demand has varied and cannot be taken at face value. Understandably incumbent governments have shown some reluctance to reform. In some cases, the response is so superficial that it is a make-believe, a bow towards rather than a genuine embrace of liberal democracy. Even if opposition parties are given a change to compete, elections may simply confirm the dominance of a particular party.

Such continuity in office is not incompatible with democracy provided it can, for example, be attributed to exceptional leadership, good fortune, modest expectations of government and slow-footed opposition. Other explanations, inimical to liberal democracy, are however more likely, for example, habitual submission to authority, a calculated submission to patrons who are part of a political network and who offer protection and occasional benefits in exchange for votes, alienation from or indifference to those in government. Conditions in Botswana have corresponded to some extent to the first set of particulars, making plausible the contention that the BDP's permanent hold on office is democratically based. In Senegal, where neither good government nor good fortune has prevailed, and even deference has become strained, any such claim is much less persuasive. The circumstances in Botswana have been exceptional, the situation in Senegal much more typical. In most of the countries embarking on multiparty politics, government remains in the hands of those introducing the reforms.

Presidential elections are most at risk of make-believe, for usually the legislature has little power and all is not lost if the president cannot count on a parliamentary majority. In Senegal, in 1993, the presidential election attracted a markedly higher turnout than did the parliamentary elections. Once Diouf had been declared elected president, the game had been lost. In Nigeria, the electoral commission was able to declare the results of the 1992 legislative elections, but was prevented from publishing those of the 1993 presidential elections. There are other examples. One more, Togo, will suffice. In the 1993 presidential election Eyadema's continuation in office was assured by the fact that none of the three main opposition leaders was a candidate. One sworn enemy, Gilchrist Olympio (his father had been murdered in the 1963 military coup led by Eyadema), was disqualified on a technicality. The other two, Kodjo and Agboyibo, withdrew rather than participate in a flawed election. The result was a walkover for Eyadema and a turnout of only 36%. For the subsequent parliamentary elections Eyadema relaxed his defiance of opposition—and international—opinion. For example, half the membership of the National Electoral Commission was representative of the opposition. As a result, the president's party, with 36 of the 81 seats, was outdistanced by the opposition. Kodjo and Agboyibo entered in to an agreement pledging mutual support so that the president would be obliged to appoint one of them prime minister. This pact did not resist the powers of the president. By persuading Kodjo to leave Agboyibo in the lurch, he was able to form his own coalition and turn an embarrassing defeat into a partial victory.

There has been, however, the occasional upset, the most notable being the defeat of President Kaunda in Zambia and that of President Kalingba in the Central African Republic. In Zambia, Kaunda, after much hesitation, decided in 1991 to lift the ban on opposition parties and to hold an election, apparently confident that, although his party might suffer a defeat in parliamentary elections, he himself would be reelected. He miscalculated in three respects. First, he was outplayed by the opposition which was much more united and resourceful than expected. The Movement for Multiparty Democracy (MMD) had brought together businessmen, strongly in favor of privatization, trade unionists resentful of official patronage, and intellectuals seeking reform but not necessarily of a liberal democratic character. The surprising display of unity when the time came to transform the movement into a political party, and especially when choosing its candidate for the presidential election, not only disconcerted Kaunda; it also contributed to divisions, hesitations and defections within his own ruling party.

Secondly, the all too familiar pressures on the electorate, from the administration and from the ruling party, virtually indistinguishable from one another, proved insufficient. They were neutralized by internally and externally based pressures which in combination tipped the scales. The internal pressures came not solely from the opposition but also from a variety of nongovernmental organizations determined to make the election a true test of public opinion. It was not always easy to distinguish them from the opposition but the nongovernmental organizations, as such, having to some extent kept themselves free of Kaunda's embrace, were careful not to become identified with the MMD, once it had become a political party contesting elections. They constituted an independent additional source of pressure on the government. This was particularly true of church and student organizations. They were closely involved in breaking the deadlock between the government and the opposition on constitutional issues. Had these not been resolved, the opposition might have boycotted the elections. Also, in cooperation with international observer teams, they ensured that the election would be effectively monitored. Zambian monitors, trained by an American observer team, were posted at all 3,489 polling stations. Their presence—and their assistance—not only improved the chances of official compliance with electoral procedures, it also reassured a hesitant electorate.

Thirdly, the judiciary, in a number of notable court cases, added its voice. It helped to ensure that emergency powers (which remained in force despite all protests from the opposition and international observers) would not be used to hamper the opposition. The courts also obliged the government-controlled media to provide a more balanced coverage of the election campaign, an obligation underlined by competition. Two independently financed newspapers were launched, one by the MMD, the other as a commercial venture.

The cumulative effect of an united opposition, internal and external cooperation in monitoring the election, an independent judiciary and freedom of the press was an election indisputably free and fair and the result equally indisputable. The opposition, with 80% of the vote, captured the presidency and assured itself of a parliamentary majority. Kaunda and his party seemed to have been taken by surprise. They accused the outside observers, shortly before polling day, of unacceptable interference, of having come to Zambia not to observe the elections but to help overthrow the government. It was too late. A Trojan horse was already inside the gates.

There are few parallels between Kaunda's defeat and that of President Kalingba in the Central African Republic, for the circumstances were altogether different. Kalingba would probably have remained in power had the French government not taken in hand in organizing fresh elections, after a false start in October 1992. These earlier elections, which had left Kalingba trailing well behind, had been annulled by the Supreme Court. Kalingba never gave up hope and tried many a trick but without French support he stood little chance. The opposition was much divided and minor opposition leaders were brought into government, indeed asked to be prime minister. But Kalingba's attempt, in June 1993, to appoint over the head of his prime minister one of his own men, with responsibility for security and other matters which could determine the outcome of an election, brought a strong and immediate reaction from the French government. Kalingba was deprived of the services of Colonel Mantion, a member of French intelligence on secondment, upon whom Kalingba relied for essential support in his bid for reelection. At the same time, the French Ambassador was replaced by a special envoy, whose task was to see that proper elections were held as soon as possible. Kalingba had little option but to acquiesce in this takeover of responsibility for the election. The country is landlocked, and the economy was in the doldrums. The government was several months behind in the payment of salaries. When Kalingba tried to stall the official declaration of results after the first round of elections, the French stigmatized this as a "veritable coup d'etat" and immediately suspended all aid. This was to deter Kalingba from proceeding any further in his resistance. No candidate had achieved an absolute majority but Kalingba was out of the running having secured only 12% of the vote. Kalingba was not so much taken by surprise as simply overruled.

Most African presidents have managed to arrange the outcome of elections more to their own advantage. The transition to multiparty politics has usually resulted in a compromise between government and opposition, between an incumbent president and a parliament in which the opposition is represented, between authoritarian and democratic practices. Elections are marred by some intimidation and by biased administration but opposition complaints are often exaggerated. The success of the ruling party is a consequence of being already in power. Many voters, and certainly officials, go with the tide, not believing it will turn in the opposition's favor, at least not decisively. The advent of contested elections involves both the government and the opposition in an assessment of their respective strengths. Either side may show intransigence or flexibility. If the opposition is divided, as is often the case, the government may consider it expedient to offer some of the opposition parties a share in power. It may seek opposition support in times of crisis. There may be factions within the ruling party which see the opposition leaders as potential allies. The opposition for its part may decide that the time has not yet come to risk an outright confrontation. The game is thus was one ins and outs, not for the dominant party which remains in place, but for opposition parties prepared to shift in and out of opposition.

The opposition claims that this is not democracy, that only if power changes hands can the system be considered democratic. It is a protest which does not take into account two possibilities. One is that a change of party in power may be no more than a substitution of one set of autocratic and corrupt politicians for another, the methods of government remaining the same. An alternation which puts in power a party concerned only with establishing its own hegemony is no improvement at all. A firm Assessment of what has been achieved, for example in Zambia and the Central African Republic, can only be made some time in the future. Both President Chiluba in Zambia and President Patasse in the Central African Republic have already shown signs of acting autocratically and of being intolerant of opposition.

The other possibility is that coalitions led by a dominant party may be the only alternative to something much worse, a retreat to entrenched positions by both sides and mutual defiance. A refusal to compromise can lead, as in Zaire, to a breakdown in government, president and parliament supporting different prime ministers, or it can result in something much worse, to civil war as in Rwanda.

In conclusion, one generalization might, after all, be ventured. A strengthening of democratic process in sub-Saharan Africa, depends to a very considerable extent upon the delicate practice of monitoring elections. This means, in present circumstances, monitoring by outside observers. This already occurs to some extent but not very convincingly. If outside observers are few in number and arrive only shortly before polling day, if the electorate is hesitant and frightened, their impact on the electoral process is minimal and their approval becomes a whitewash. Even if their report is critical, it comes too late as in the 1993 Togo presidential election. Monitoring, to be effective, needs to be preventative, that is begin early, probe deeply into the whole electoral process and seek to remedy in good time whatever defects appear. This is, of course, interference in a country's internal affairs, welcomed by those in opposition, discouraged by those in power, but a justifiable test of the government's readiness to see liberal democratic procedures enforced—its willingness as well as its capacity.

CHAPTER 5

LIBERAL DEMOCRACY FOR SOUTH AFRICA?

Sam C. Nolutshungu

INTRODUCTION

In 1994, after 46 years of apartheid, South Africa held its first democratic, non-racial election. The once exiled African National Congress under the leadership of Nelson Mandela won more than three-fifths of the popular vote and took power at the head of a multiparty coalition. Four years of negotiations marked by large-scale, persistent, atrocious violence in which some 15,000 people were killed, culminated in a change of government accepted by all but a minority of white extremists. Political violence diminished and outside of politics, economic life continued much as before. True, there were wage demands backed by dramatic strike action which was widely reported as signalling an explosion of risen expectations among blacks that were not being fulfilled. But there was nothing new in workers' activism, and it certainly did not signal an economic revolution. The white minority suffered no loss of its well-being and faced no marked deterioration of its security. To be sure, the spectacular growth of armed criminality created personal insecurity for all, especially in the large urban areas, but that was largely the consequence of the social conditions of mass unemployment created by apartheid, the failure of its institutions of governance and social control, and the proliferation of firearms as the result of its regional wars. There was a widely shared hope that a popularly elected government, enjoying greater legitimacy would be in a better position to act decisively against crime, even though so much would depend on the delivery of economic improvement to the sprawling black townships which was by no means assured.

In the mixture of inter-party negotiation and legitimation politics of the period since 1990, there was a definite popular-ization of democratic themes—regarding rights, institutions and procedures—and a rhetoric of common belonging and common purpose within a democratic polity emerged. Yet, even as the ANC continued to stress wide consultation and consensus in its reconstruction policies and as a matter of political style and strategy, there was some tension between its radical, latterly, populist heritage and the accommodation of the old elites. Leaders gravitated toward notions of democracy that were far less populist or radical than those that had animated the movement that had forced the apartheid regime to negotiate. The deradicalization of the apartheid movement was the price of a deal with its erstwhile enemy but also the *sine qua non* of Western investments, loans and aid.

The transitional constitutional agreements reflected the continuing power of the old order and of the privileged sections of the population—the enforced coalition govern-ment desired by them but not by the majority of the ANC, guarantees of employment to the entire apartheid public service, and commitments to conservative economic policies diametrically opposed to what the ANC and its communist ally had once championed. A federal system, insisted upon by the white elite, replaced the old tribal homelands of apartheid giving universal citizenship to all South Africans but there was

120

some fear that the new division had the potential of forming the basis of new fiefdoms for politicians who chose to rely on race and ethnic identities for support.

In the first year cooperation between the new government and the old economic and political elites was real. Despite major problems in the attempted integration of former guerrillas into the armed forces and the deracialization of the public service the machinery of the state yielded by and large to the change of leadership—no mutinies and no mass resignations.

Peace was achieved through a policy reconciliation which gave legitimacy to the continuance of inherited institutions, advocated cautious change brought about in the least provocative ways as through the Reconstruction and Development Programme endorsed by all the political parties. The new government was committed to a restitution of some of the land seized from blacks under the previous regime and a reconstruction levy was imposed to pay for some amelioration for the black population, but the effect of the agreements with the old regime and its supporters amounted to "What you have you keep."

The magnanimous gesture was part of the spirit of reconciliation acclaimed throughout the world. The question was who should pay for it.[1] The vast economic inequality between white and black and the limited scope for reducing it under the economic strategies deemed possible, the continued physical segregation of populations with its effect of perpetuating inequality and the excitement of racial passions among non-Africans, by demands for redress made by the victims of apartheid and, among Africans, by the resistance to such claims—all these remained as pressing challenges for the new democracy. Black and white leaders agreed that economic growth based on massive inflows of foreign capital was essential for political stability. Yet, what if such flows failed to materialize? In any event, foreign investment was less likely to be attracted if the government placed equity before profit in its economic interventions. Indeed, both the previously interventionist National Party of De Klerk and the entire white economic elite insisted on a conception of liberal democracy that was political in the narrowest sense with minimum levelling power, in contrast to the ANC's emphasis on a consensual approach to development that moderates the effect of "the market." The threat of violent subversion from the extreme right together with the continuing political violence in rural Natal, in the context of a high level of armed criminality everywhere, was a continual reminder that the relative peace which prevailed could not be taken for granted. It was only too evident that the victory against apartheid—great as any achievement in modern politics—was partial and, in the nature of these things, still vulnerable to reaction and the effects of the crushing burden of the past.

The test of whether democracy had come to stay would be set by the next elections, not merely the local government ones that were scheduled for late 1995—important as those were likely to be both by their conduct and their results—but by the next general elections under new rules and a revised constitution still to be fashioned out. But hope was, emphatically, well justified, not least by the sheer difficulty of envisaging the configuration of power that could work apart from it in the present and immediate future.

The discussion which follows and which makes up the rest of this chapter was written before the release of Nelson Mandela and the repatriation of the exiled ANC, before the protracted negotiation process that produced the interim constitution and the freedom elections. It now serves as a flashback—a record of how the prospects of democracy appeared in 1989—in a time characterized as one of stalemate between the apartheid regime and the mass movement which challenged it. There may be some interest in seeing how different or how similar things appeared then and in judging how the enduring questions are beginning to be answered and abiding fears allayed or deepened.

122

LIBERAL DEMOCRACY FOR SOUTH AFRICA?

To discuss democracy in South Africa is to talk about the future, about hopes and fears. Little in the present or the past promises the success of any such thing, yet people want democracy and many believe it is the only possible solution to the problem of coexistence within one country of common citizenship, of white and black, rich and poor South Africans not in spite of but because of their history. What follows are some preliminary reflections on the major areas of difficulty, but also on the seemingly improbable grounds for hope. Our subject cannot be whether democracy as a ready-made system, once-agreed and decided upon, can prosper on such ground, but whether democratization can securely advance as a process with a duration in time that cannot be predicted but the measure of whose success is its steady progress through the foreseeable setbacks and pitfalls towards its aim.

There are two problems which are related but which should not be confused. One is of the short-term and the other not: namely, whether it is probable that a democratic constitution of some kind might be agreed upon among the parties as a means of ending apartheid, and the larger question of whether a democracy, once agreed as a device to end apartheid—analogous in this respect to many independent constitutions which functioned simply to 'turn a key' but were not intended by anyone to be followed afterward—can subsequently be given substance in a genuine process of democratization.

It seems incontrovertible that if a negotiated end of apartheid were achieved it would be on the basis of a more or less democratic constitution. The government has declared itself in favor of democracy though subject to guarantees for minorities and for private enterprise. The African National Congress has published Constitutional Guidelines and an Interim Constitutional Framework that are firmly democratic in aim. How far the agreement for the ending of apartheid involves agreement on democratic rights and procedures for the future, and to what extent the agreement itself is reached in ways that are generally accepted as democratic will, no doubt, influence subsequent political development. But the task of constructing a democracy only begins with the transfer of power and initiates a process that can only work itself out fully after apartheid. Democratic construction goes well beyond what may be termed the 'constitutional moment' of designing, negotiating and adopting a constitution. Indeed, the constitution itself cannot be democratic for long if it cannot evolve beyond the initial moment when its overriding function is to facilitate a single event: the transfer of power rather than to mastery of the consequences of that event as they subsequently unfold.

MOVEMENT TOWARD DEMOCRACY

That there has been a long struggle for democracy in South Africa admits of little doubt.[2] Equally, it is evident that this movement is deeply rooted in popular experience of white rule. While at one time, up to the middle to late 1950s, democratization was widely expected to take the form of the progressive extension of the rights and liberties enjoyed by whites under the racially exclusive democracy instituted under British auspices in 1910, it is now equally widely felt that the creation of a democracy in South Africa would be a radical departure, going well beyond any mere adaptation or reform of a system designed for white domination.

That is all the more so since, having stifled any possibility of growth towards fuller freedom and democracy by the imposition of an iron grid of police state laws, the white oligarchy itself began in the 1980s to dismantle the 1910 constitutional order in favor of a less democratic if, marginally, more multiracial one by the addition of Colored and Indian Houses elected under separate voters' roles, the suppression of the Senate, the imposition of a strong presidentialism (supported by a multiracial President's Council) and, under P. W. Botha, the increased involvement of the military in government.[3] .

To be sure, if democracy of any kind is ever achieved, it is most unlikely that the traces of the earlier racialist democracy will be totally effaced: survivals may be expected to remain in various institutional domains in very much the same way that postcolonial states in the rest of Africa recognizably bear the marks of the colonial orders to which they succeeded, both in their institutions and, to a greater degree than is commonly acknowledged, legal and constitutional practice and political culture generally.[4] The distribution of social and economic power, even among the previously voteless blacks, will continue for years to reflect not only their different economic fortunes under the old order but their roles in its system of domination and repression. The compromises that produce a negotiated constitutional settlement by their nature involve a measure of accommodation between the new political forces and the old, and legitimation of some elements of the architecture of power and privilege bequeathed by the old order.

From the point of view of democratic construction as an evolutionary process, power and privilege do not stand as a categoric antithesis to democracy. The consolidation of state power, which is a prerequisite for a democratic as for any political order, is rooted in the ordering of inequality. The growth of rights and the limitation of state power have their roots in the resistance of privileged classes and strata to threats which state consolidation poses to their position and wealth. Just as the privileged English-speaking population, especially its financial magnates, placed some restraints on the exercise of Afrikaner nationalist power, so too, the Afrikaner power bloc which has assimilated them and, in subordinate roles, various categories of blacks as well are poised to limit state power under black majority rule and to insist upon their 'entitlements', appealing for wider support by using the language of 'rights'.

Nevertheless, it is from the movements of opposition—liberal, nationalist, and socialist—to the 'white democracy' that the positive impetus for democratization emerges, and it is on their ideas and practices that the prospects of successful democratic construction are seen to rest. Except among small minorities of intellectuals, the resistance of the whites to the state has never taken the form of an advocacy of universal rights that might entitle blacks to participation in a nonracial democracy. By and large, the rights of blacks have been little advanced by the struggles of the different categories of whites for their own rights. On the contrary, the extension of political rights was perceived as a threat to disadvantaged whites who could only get to participate in racial privilege by the denial of blacks' rights. If, in recent years, faced with the failures of state policy, black revolt, and international opposition, some of the more well-to-do whites have urged political reform, their embrace of democracy is not unqualified by a desire to conserve their material achievements under apartheid.

The demand for democracy has emerged most strongly from the movements of the oppressed though their conceptions of rights and political democracy have often been implicit in their struggle rather than explicitly formulated as such. It is to such movements that increasing numbers of people, both in South Africa and abroad, have looked for a definition of the political character of a post-apartheid South Africa and specifically, in recent years, the constitutional basis of a democratic succession. Hence, the stream of white delegations to the ANC's Lusaka headquarters following the upheavals of the middle 1980s, to seek authoritative indications about how the interests of whites would fare under a changed order.

Both whites and blacks, both the privileged and the oppressed, have invoked democratic principles, at various stages of South African history, both to gain power and to limit its exercise: for whites, to protect acquired rights and privileges and for blacks to gain new ones or, at the limit of ideological imagination, to recover ones that were once held in a pre-colonial past, or once promised in an earlier phase of white rule. In different ways, and to differing degrees among the two camps, the concept of democracy has been both conservative and progressive.

It is simply impossible in South Africa, or anywhere else for that matter, to associate democracy only with new creation and the obliteration of the past, as it is to found it on a restoration or a revalorization of past achievements and entitlements alone. Both radicals and conservatives can claim a part of it, and it is, probably, what else they want in addition to democracy that may decide whether their claims can be accommodated or reconciled.[5]

It is, of course, important to bear in mind that the central issue of South African politics has been racial domination, and democracy has arisen as an ideal in opposition to it, but not always as the only one, or the only way of conceiving of the world to come after apartheid. Within the black nationalist movement and among white radicals, democracy has often given way to a greater emphasis on socialist aims, frequently being referred to as a stage—the 'national democratic' stage—on the road to socialism, necessary but transitional.[6] For many Marxists, national democracy implied class compromise and a partial victory to be completed only with the creation of socialism. Among white moderates, who also considered themselves to be realists, the removal of racial discrimination without full democracy but under some system of 'power sharing' or an oligarchy united by class interests, has often seemed a more 'realistic' outcome to hope for.

The currents of opinion have changed in response to developments within the country and to international influences, including the varying ideological force of democratic ideals within other societies. Yet if at any stage opposition movements were called upon to state in political terms their griefs and their hopes, it would predominantly have been in terms of democracy even if this was ideologically labeled as transitional. There are many reasons for this which we cannot now explore, but it may help to note a few. Undemocratic government, especially racial tyranny, calls forth democratic aspirations in opposition to itself. The language of such demands is universal, while the claims themselves are practically impossible to discredit in our time. Second, democracy-for-whites automatically placed democracy-for-all on the historical agenda, all the more so as the illusion of its likely evolution into a multiracial or more inclusive system was maintained for long against the background of the colonial pseudo-democracies of the Cape and Natal which were supplanted by the 1910 Act. Third, almost all the injustices suffered by blacks were compounded by their exclusion from political power, and political objectives, most powerfully represented in the idea of universal enfranchisement, were immediately understood and were potentially more unifying than any other ideal which relied on a specific theory or ideology—such as marxism or liberalism rigorously conceived.

Above all, at crucial historical moments when mass mobilization has been at a premium, and the need was felt to unite the forces opposed to apartheid, the language and aims of democracy have been paramount. That was the case at Kliptown in 1956 where the Freedom Charter was drawn up as a democratic document that could unite white radicals and black nationalists, and in 1983-1984 when it was judged necessary to mount a broad front of opposition to Botha's constitutional reforms and the United Democratic Front was formed.

It was with Botha's counterdemocratic reforms and the emergence of the United Democratic Front that there emerged in 1984-86 a mass democratic struggle, conscious of itself as such, of a scale and intensity without precedent in Africa, and one of the most remarkable of this century anywhere.

The events that followed raised several vexing questions, namely, whether mass democratic struggles accelerate the process of such transformation, whether they hinder or help it, and whether they are compatible with a negotiated accommodation which appears to be the only alternative to revolution or a 'hurting stalemate'. Or, to put the same question somewhat differently, whether democracy comparable to the kinds obtaining in the advanced industrial countries of the West is compatible with militant agitation. Equally, many within the mass democratic movement, as it has come to be known, have wondered whether any negotiated settlement will not necessarily signify a betrayal of the very aspects of the struggle, popular and radical, that gave it moral force and political effectiveness. Negotiated settlements for the transfer of power in Africa (including that of Zimbabwe which is often perceived in the West as a model of successful mediation and negotiation) are widely seen in this light within Southern Africa itself.

A much more difficult question related to the process of struggle and its compatibility with the creation of liberal-democratic institutions. It recalls one that was often raised at the beginning of modern democracy: whether 'liberty' (and property) could be secured under democracy, and whether the agitation of the masses led inevitably, via mob rule, to tyranny. Though, for the most part, settled by subsequent history in the case of the Western democracies, the issue still has a gripping reality for privileged classes in countries where democracies are still being, or to be, constructed. In South Africa's recent history it has been raised with a certain poignancy by the developments within the popular movement at the height of its agitation.

The struggle which emerged to challenger Botha's reform was a democratic one in many senses. It specifically articulated its demands as democratic ones, seeking universal citizenship and enfranchisement, with a strong emphasis on civil rights. In this way, it was neither ethnic nor racial, but showed a marked shift from the traditional African nationalist focus of black movements. While many of its activists would have seen themselves as socialists, the UDF and all the organisms that emerged in its wake placed less emphasis on class differences among the majority population, or indeed among whites: they saw the fight in terms of one that pitted the people against the state and its collaborators: populist, and preeminently political, even while increasingly presenting the state as serving the interest of capital. In other words, they subsumed the economic in the political, and in the struggle against the state strategically blurred the boundaries of class.[7]

The movement was decentralized, the UDF itself loosely confederating some 600 voluntary associations across the country which retained their local character and initiative.[8] Within them there emerged a strong emphasis on democratic decision making, a trend influenced by developments within the trade union movement which soon became a major part of the resistance to the racist reforms. The unions became for many a source and a model of organizational thought. They also raised among the people at large a stronger awareness of the black working class as a political force and of the predominately working class character of the African population.[9] That gave great currency to notions of democracy embodying distinctly socialist rather than liberal values.[10] Democracy was meant to put an end to racial oppression but also to curb economic exploitation and to bring about a redistribution of wealth and a general improvement of living conditions for blacks. It was meant to apply to all areas of life, including the school and the workplace. In the height of the unrest, many looked to the trade union movement to provide political leadership and when it did, between 1986 and 1987, its role was widely welcomed.

The events of the years of intense struggle have been widely recounted and it would serve little purpose to review them here, except to recall the aspects most relevant to present themes.[11]

Every avenue of protest was explored, from the use of economic power in consumer boycotts, to strikes and the withholding of rent payments on council houses: schools were boycotted by children who saw no point in 'education before liberation' considering that the education provided by the state was of little practical or intellectual value. The protests were countrywide and, significantly, involved high levels of protest in both the rural and urban areas over the same period, something which had proved extremely difficult to achieve in the past. This reflected not only superior organization and better access to the means of communication than had been possible before, though undoubtedly these were important factors, but the extent of the crisis. State authority had broken down at virtually all points of contact with the black population and the simultaneity of intense discontent over a diversity of issues, local as well as national, in the Bantustans as well as in what used to be called 'white South Africa'.

The confrontation between the democratic movement and the forces of the state, now involving direct participation of the military in 'law and order' functions in the townships, produced a level of state violence quite unequaled even in South Africa's long history of bloody suppression.

It is a fact of the first importance in understanding the development of the process of mass democratic struggle to recognize fully the context of state violence—the use of collaborators, and the application of psychological pressures on children and young people in detention to turn them into collaborators—and its contribution to the climate of violence which, for a while, prevailed among blacks themselves.

The conflict between collaborators and protestors produced the phenomenon of the 'necklace', originated by young radicals but soon adopted by collaborators and *agents provacateurs* paid or blackmailed by the state to terrorize their former comrades and to sow confusion within the mass movement. Above all, there was an outbreak of a many-sided violent conflict in Natal between Mpondo and Zulu, Zulu and Indian communities, as well as a virtual war between UDF supporters and the state-supported Inkatha movement of Chief Gatsha Buthelezi. Within the democratic movement, cleavages between the UDF with predominantly ANC sympathies, called 'Charterists' (after the Freedom Charter to which they subscribed), and the black-power-minded adherents of Azapo and the National Forum also produced violent confrontation.

The capacity of the national leadership to control the militants at the local level was limited. Street committees, as an exercise in 'direct democracy', tried to perform some of the functions of government, undertaking judicial as well as administrative functions. But they were not equal to the task without coordination by more experienced political leadership and they were subject to harassment by the state. Neither the UDF, because of its structure and the constraints imposed upon it by state repression, nor the ANC leadership based outside the country, could respond with sufficient alacrity to control events. There was a danger of popular disillusion, provoked by an incipient violent anarchy, and scope enough for the state to regain the initiative and, with its collaborators, to fight back.

When the people rushed upon the political stage, they brought with them all their weaknesses as well as their strengths in political understanding and organization, in their fears and resentments, their urgent hopes and pent-up frustrations. They also showed the political incohesion of communities among whom democratic mobilization had been prevented over many years and political opinion had been forced to become episodic, cryptic and even peremptory.

It was a measure of the capacity of those communities to produce leaders and the authority of those leaders that, in most areas (except Natal), the drift towards anarchic violence and ultra-leftism among the youth was eventually restrained by patient persuasion and negotiation.

At the level of ideology, there were contradictory developments. Radical and even revolutionary ideas gained considerable currency, particularly among workers' organizations and among the young. On the other hand, the idea of a broad front of opposition on the basis of democratic demands signified a retreat from some traditional positions of the liberation movement, particularly those influenced by Leninism and Maoism. However, democracy and the struggle for it were conceived in socially radical terms. For once, popular, nationalist, and socialist groups who had tended to be skeptical of 'mere democracy' without socialism reclaimed democratic discourse from its association with the 'bourgeoisie' and with 'liberals'.

In practical politics, the mass struggles also produced contradictory results. On the one hand, they provoked repression signified by the declaration of a state of emergency periodically renewed for the rest of Botha's ministry, and a growth of antidemocratic extremism among whites. On the other hand, they stimulated a significant proportion of white middle class opinion, including notable Afrikaners, to seek accommodation with the democratic movement.

Apart from the manifest inability of the Botha government to bring an end to the black revolt, or contain political violence, or even to ensure the security of its collaborators whose own behavior increased lawlessness and feuding in the townships, the state was unable to proffer any credible solution to a whole range of other crises: housing, unemployment, shortages of skilled workers, external sanctions and foreign investment, a high level of public expenditure due to the attempt to hold on to Namibia, and wars of destabilization against neighboring countries which were part of Botha's total strategy.

Emergency regulations, press censorship, detentions and violent attacks on activists by state-sponsored vigilantes, subdued the agitation but did not defeat the movement. A permanent leadership had emerged, linking community leaders, union organizers, and churchpeople with the political organizations, particularly the ANC, in varying degrees of closeness of cooperation and affiliation.

The effect on the white population of Botha's reform ministry, its turbulent repudiation by blacks, and its violent involution, was a general loss of assurance. Significant sections of the elite became dissatisfied with Botha's attempts to find solutions along the lines of a reformed apartheid; many sought an opening too genuinely representative of black organizations and leaders. Others, like the Conservative party of Dr. Andries Treurnicht blamed Botha's reforms and favored a less ambiguous defense of white supremacy. The vast majority of Afrikaners remained faithful to the National party. Yet many did so in the belief that the government could still find a solution other than a simple reaffirmation of white supremacy, segregation and discrimination. Thought gravitated toward the protection, in a South Africa that was bound to become multiracial, of Afrikaner 'identity and culture' (and, no doubt, the material gains that Afrikaners had made under apartheid).[12]

Of those business people, clergy, intellectuals and athletes who sought drastic reform, few believed that it could be achieved on any basis other than a common citizenship for all and the complete end of legal discrimination. None favored, in public at any rate, an authoritarian solution, however multiracial it might appear to be. Such a thing would simply not gain acceptance at home or abroad. It is, perhaps, fair to say that for a significant portion of the white elite, fear of democracy was matched by a declining faith in the system of government that had served them so well. Many came to believe that the present state could not be made to function well and advantageously without an extension of freedom and democracy (we leave aside the question of just how much democracy or freedom they had in mind). Not only were these necessary to end the isolation of the country and to attract greatly needed foreign investment; they were also needed to enable the domestic economy to operate without bottlenecks of labor supply, artificial restrictions of trade and growth, and continual industrial strife.

Many began to take seriously the prospect of an eventual ANC succession to the Nationalist government. While moving towards accommodation with the democratic movement, major economic interests, like those represented by the mining giant Anglo-American, advertised their differences with the apartheid regime, while seeking assurances that a future ANC government would not pursue nationalization and 'confiscatory taxation'. Many white intellectuals—and not only those traditionally associated with English-speaking liberalism—sought guarantees for civil liberties, calling for a Bill of Rights for South Africa, now no longer to curb apartheid, believed to be on its way out, but to bind its anticipated successors and those who supported them.

POLITICAL INTEREST GROUPS

If a consensus was emerging within the opposition to apartheid about the necessity of democracy, there were nonetheless important differences in the way it was seen, reflecting diverse class interests and the ideologies which had historically been adopted to articulate them. For liberals, democracy was essentially a political and legal problem which would practically be solved once civil rights, under the rule of law, replaced apartheid and its discriminatory and repressive legislation. For Marxists and radical nationalists, economic exploitation and oppression were central and little would be achieved if the oppressed were not empowered to work effectively for their elimination.

The cleavage between those with a purely political or juridical concept of democracy and those who approved it for its content or consequences of economic amelioration was an old one and not unique to South Africa. It was complicated there, by the coincidence of race and class, and by the vast differences of economic situations as well as by the radical form the conflict had assumed.

In seeking the destruction of the political order, disadvantaged groups also challenged the legitimacy of the economic order; in seeking political power they intended to use it to tip the balance of economic advantage in their favor as other classes have done before them. All the major black movements had workers or peasants as their mass base even at times when their leaders were decidedly 'petit bourgeois' in fact as well as in ideological orientation. They readily evolved towards more or less socialist ways of seeing racial oppression. The impact of communists on working class struggles in the 1940s, and their willingness to ally themselves with the nationalist movement, reinforced the class emphasis in black struggles. Western support for the white regimes during the Cold War gave considerable purchase to such a view. The armed struggle begun in 1959 and the eclipse of liberalism (never strong) in the late 1960s and 1970s, together with developments in the rest of the world, gained Marxism (often without party affiliation) considerable influence among young intellectuals, both white and black. This experience could not simply be brushed aside in the construction of democracy. It had become a part of the collective memory and Marxist ideas were a permanent element in the political culture. Democracy was associated by most people with economic improvement through state intervention and the redistribution of wealth and property. In its 'Constitutional Guidelines' the ANC declared in favor of a "mixed economy."

Afrikaner nationalism had already established the precedent of extensive state intervention and social welfare for a disadvantaged section of the white population. Promising improvement to the disadvantaged Afrikaners, and using the state to promote the growth of Afrikaner capital, it was firmly opposed to economic laissez-faire. Although perceptions of the economic character of the desired democracy vary within the mass movement—especially on the role of the state in promoting black entrepreneurship—the predominant view is that the primary duty is to ensure state intervention to improve and empower the popular classes.

In itself this emphasis need not make impossible pragmatic collaboration between liberal and socialist democrats over the immediate problem of removing apartheid. The democratic movement straddles the two positions, in any event. However, the manner in which it may be represented in a post-apartheid constitution, the extent of redistribution and of the power of the state to intervene, are already matters of important controversy. Furthermore, the dynamic process of redressing the problems of inequality—as through differential provision in education, employment (especially in the public sector) and the question of assistance to black enterprises and the cooperatives envisaged by the ANC—is likely to prove contentious. At a more fundamental social level, the balance between working class interests and those of capital in the constitution and the political institutions that flow from it are matters on which there is deep division even though positions have yet to be stated clearly in terms of constitutional principles.

The question of whether there would be wholesale nationalization of major enterprises dominated political debate in the first few months following the unbanning of the ANC and the Communist party, made urgent by two contradictory developments. On the one hand there was the growth in popularity of socialist ideas and of the Communist party itself among young militants and in the trade unions; on the other, the crisis of socialism in the West and the collapse of communism in the East. In practice, the response of both the ANC and the CP was to retreat from any nationalization as a key commitment in economic affairs without, however, completely renouncing it.

While nationalization and traditional Marxist ideas of directive planning could no longer be championed with clarity, all progressive movements were confronted with the extraordinary distortions in South Africa's development: unusually high differences of wealth and widespread poverty previously sustained by racialist legislation and an authoritarian state; vast discrepancies in the levels of economic development between sectors and regions; the dominance of oligopolies in the key sectors of mining, industry, and finance; and, as regards social welfare, a massive backlog of ameliorative tasks in black education, housing, health and nutrition. It seemed wholly unlikely that any black government would be tolerated by its followers to leave all these problems to 'the market' to resolve. If, in recognition of the problems of socialist planning in a hostile international climate, a successor black government demurred, could it sustain political tranquility without recourse to authoritarian measures against its former militants, including the labor unions? This pointed to a major problem of legitimation that would face any government that succeeds to the apartheid regime.

Many militants recognized that however much socialism been discredited by Soviet failures, it had never been a mere will-o'-the-wisp, but had arisen as a response to very real problems of economic development for which no other system had provided any better solutions. Yet no one seemed to know, and certainly no one said with clarity, quite what might be salvaged with advantage from that experience, and how.

If traditional liberals emphasize the rights of individuals and the security of private enterprise as a condition favoring their enjoyment, reformist Afrikaner intellectuals are more sensitive to questions of 'group rights' by which they signal a concern for the fate of Afrikaners as such in a changed order. Although this is typically advertised as a cultural concern, it is sustained by a sense of economic insecurity within a category that has traditionally been able to rely on a considerable amount of economic protection and assistance by the state. Yet the issue of 'group rights' is not entirely a matter of ethnic special pleading. Although its full importance and relevance to democracy is obscured by the predominantly antidemocratic context of official thinking with which it is generally associated, it had many complex aspects that are crucial to the project of democracy.

LIBERAL DEMOCRACY FOR SOUTH AFRICA?

It is simply impossible in a society governed in a racist way for so long, in which personal identity was officially defined racially and ethnically, for the basic human interests of all persons, and not only the most privileged, to be advanced without reference to their perceived communal identities. While 'no-go areas' for democracy and integration would be hard to justify and impossible to enforce, there is ample room for debate about 'collective rights' and what they might mean. The most obvious application of the concept is in the domain of cultural provisions in the constitution and cultural policy generally, but for other groups its meaning may be essentially economic.

The problem of legitimacy will pose itself in a different way from the perspective of those who feel defeated, and yet it is no less genuine and deserving of attention for that. It ought to be possible to distinguish between reaction, on the one hand, and well-founded concerns of minorities about the conditions under which they give their loyalty and service to the state, between conservatism (even tainted with racism) and mere subversion. It ought to be possible to make the distinction from both sides, of governors and governed. If it is not, then democracy itself is impossible, because a minimum consensus is unattainable.

The clamor for "group rights," perhaps inadvertently, highlights the inadequacy of viewing citizens exclusively as individuals without regard to collectivities and the collective or communitarian contexts in which those rights may be exercised. The argument could conceivably be thrown back by radical black movements as a claim for collective amelioration of racial 'groups' previously collectively disadvantaged and for a substantial inflexion of the 'rights of individuals' insofar as these protect unequal distribution of income and wealth.

The existence of collective rights to land, the periodic conflicts among herding communities, and the threats to property and to the quality of the environment in poorer areas provide examples where persons cannot advance their own interest or well-being individually. The ANC's own promise of a workers' charter to be appended to the constitution, comparable to the proposed European 'Social Charter' is, in principle, a recognition of such rights.

However, there are insuperable problems with "group rights" when taken to mean the rights of "races" and "ethnic groups"—the foundations of the very system that everyone now wishes to abolish. These highly reified concepts are virtually impossible to separate from the ideologies of racism and tribalism. Nor does it seem at all practical that the more odious practice of racial classification of persons could inoffensively be replaced with an elective system of ethnic classification in such a way that the rights of those Afrikaners who wanted to remain 'group' could be guaranteed in a democratic constitution along with those of various black ethnic groups also voluntarily joined. It would be evident to all but the most credulous that it was, in fact, the racial purpose of preventing *black* majorities from successfully electing governments which such a redefinition would be intended to serve. It is of some interest that the idea of group rights has not enjoyed any popularity among *non-Afrikaner* minorities.

It is true, nevertheless, that interests that are perceived as pertaining to certain collectivities and their right to develop a sense of identity and to agitate in politics for their perceived interests cannot properly be ignored in any democracy. It may be that collective rights amount to no more than the right to secure the conditions for a socially distinguishable (or self-distinguishing) category of persons under which its individual members can enjoy the same rights as other individuals in the wider society.

In principle, *liberal*-democracy can comprehend all these conceptions of rights or at any rate provide a framework in which they can fruitfully contend; and in the making of a democratic constitution for South Africa, it may well be possible to secure broad agreement on some version of each. It is unlikely that democracy would fail because of differences between parties or movements over fundamental rights issues. However, problems may arise in relation to the confidence that various parties may have in their rivals' ability to adhere to even their own concepts of rights with consistent good faith. In other words, political behavior and policy action interpreted from one or other rights perspective are likely to be the main areas of difficulty. The policy problems that will arise from the vast economic inequalities between classes, and between black and white, especially in times of recession or slow growth, are intractable: efforts to redress or to conserve them will determine behavior options that are often at the margin of liberal toleration. Differences over conceptions of rights now serve as indicators of the ideological (and, therefore, class) perspectives from which such future crises will be approached. In that sense, it is important how those differences are evaluated, and what valuation any agreed constitutional and institutional framework may make possible.

There is a view that racial and ethnic sentiment in a deeply divided South Africa would automatically produce a degree of suspicion, tension and violence that no democracy could cope with. It is difficult to see the basis of this expectation since in all cases where endemic communal conflict (ethnic, racial, religious) has supplanted democracy, there have been other things that were more decisive for the failure of democracy. They have included problems of the economic relations between groups, but even more intractable, that of the distribution of political power which in many cases only seemed to be democratic or was qualified by 'collective' and 'consociational' arrangements that would themselves, under quite predictable circumstances, be a source of violent strife not about the working of democracy but over whether what obtained was democratic at all.[13] The important question is how racial sentiment and identities are mobilized and the nature of the democracy itself, particularly the extent to which it is designed to accept or resist adaptation to the diverse demands of society.

LIBERAL DEMOCRACY IN NON-WESTERN STATES

There is scant evidence to show that ethnic and racial antagonisms are more threatening to democracy than to other forms of rule, or that democracies cope in less satisfactory ways with them. In its extreme manifestation opposition often threatens not the form of rule, but the existence of the state itself as a single entity. Where secession is sought or exists as a practical option, its champions are seldom discouraged by mere democracy, though democratic systems may marginally be better able to cope with, or even to yield peacefully to, separatist claims.

Despite the centrality of racial oppression, political movements in South Africa are divided over ideological and policy issues that are not comprehended by racial identity alone. Moreover, the predominant black movements have for decades been committed to an antiracism which was more than a mere negation of white rule but an insistence on the possibility and desirability of an inclusive South African citizenship transcending race. That will count for something in the days ahead.

While it is true that democracy would mean that the whites could never again rule alone or through a white party, it is nevertheless not true that their interests as individuals or as members of classes would necessarily be underrepresented. The diversity of opinion among blacks, as well as their conflicting class interests, should make possible political alliances that can effectively obviate such an outcome.

It emerged quite clearly from the struggles of the mid-1980s, from the behavior of 'collaborators' and Bantustan leaders who felt embattled—and who in several cases turned towards violent methods of suppressing the democratic movement in their own domains—that even apartheid has reliable allies whose own political interests make them much more than mere collaborators. The KwaZulu Indaba, intended to achieve a separate (if partial) solution for Gatsha Buthelezi and the Natal whites while guaranteeing the province maximum autonomy in any majority rule settlement, received the cautious encouragement of Pretoria. Despite pleas from various quarters, the central government has been unwilling to act forcefully to restrain the KwaZula Inkatha movement or to halt some Bantustan leaders who have associated themselves with the ANC. Those who benefitted by the policy of 'separate development' may well be attracted to an alliance with the National party either during the transfer of power or in the future. This applies as much to those who manned the 'Indian' and 'Colored' structures of collaboration as it does to their African counterparts. There is no party that can give satisfaction to all in the measure of their expectations, and, in a multiparty system, no black party could completely rule out, indefinitely, the option of alignment with a conservative white bloc with substantial white support, resources and money—all the more so if its share of the future black vote was insufficient to carry it to office.

Here, racism does, however, create problems. The black collaborators may fear the radical movement but they do not approve of racism, while at present the National party represents nothing apart from the racial defense of white privilege that other parties might not champion more effectively. The popular support of Bantustan leaders, such as it is, would quickly melt away once the National party could no longer guarantee them in power by force if they were identified with its racial conservatism. The National party's white followers, for their part, would not be much comforted by such an alliance. They are not likely to place their trust in black princes.

For the National party itself, the option of mobilizing the old Bantustan structures is not without its own difficulties. It falls on the National party to prepare the transfer of power to a post-apartheid regime. In the process, it must convince its former supporters that racism has no further role to play, and the black majority population that it is now fully committed to a nonracial democracy. It must create the conditions for apartheid's enemies to come to power and maintain a framework of civil order for that to happen in peaceful conditions. That limits the extent to which it can shore up by underhanded means Bantustan oligarchies when they face popular repudiation, or tolerate a partisan use of force which threatens to provoke civil war. On the other hand, it is obliged to cooperate with the ANC-SACP, forming in effect, a coalition with them against whatever threatens a negotiated democratic resolution of the problem of apartheid. Depending on how that project unfolds, and on how its opponents fare and behave, cooperation between the National party and its former enemies may grow to make it impossible to reestablish the old alliances without significant modifications that may divide both the National party and the Bantustan leaders previously allied to it. Indeed, some of the Bantustan leaders, despairing of Pretoria's vacillations, may be drawn into alliances with the white 'ultra-right' in its various forms to disrupt the transfer of power and to secure a territorial division of power in order to hold onto some of their power and privilege. That would be all the more likely to be the case if opposition movements among blacks became even more violent and if ultra-right elements, with the help of sections of the security forces, were to opt to systematic violent destabilization of the transfer process.

In short, there is a considerable fluidity in party politics and practical consideration of power modify at every stage the logic of racial identity and assertion, for blacks as well as whites. That may produce instability but, provided that political violence can be effectively restrained, it is also the very stuff of democratic politics.

Meanwhile, theoreticians of the National party have, for some time, focussed their attention on a solution that would assure political participation to all races but would reduce Afrikaners (or the National party) to a minority status in political terms and would not oblige Afrikaners to become integrated socially and culturally with other people. Plans for a racial federation, or confederation, were entertained but they ran into the predictable difficulty that they would only protect the Afrikaners from minority status if the votes of all the other groups were heavily deflated, that is, if 'democracy' amounted to something less than one man, one vote, or mechanisms were found to neutralize the effect, under a universal suffrage, of the preponderance of blacks, some 27 million over the five or so million whites.

The problem for the ruling party is the virtual certainty that any credible system of democracy would spell the end of the National party as a party of government: it would amount to abdication. To be sure, alliances could be constructed with black collaborators, all the more so under some imaginable federal arrangements, but these would be shifting coalitions in which the dominance of the National party could hardly be assured, given the greater number of supporters its partners would have to command to make the coalition worthwhile.

Now, abdication is not inconceivable. Ian Smith did it in Rhodesia in favor of a free Zimbabwe. But it becomes much easier to think about it and about its terms, and to purvey them to one's followers, when the alternatives have become obviously unbearable and the present itself untenable. In many ways a protracted period of negotiation with the ANC-SACP during which mass protest among blacks was suspended, or the formations that made possible grass roots rebellion were dissolved, or the black movement dissipated its energies in internecine conflict, could encourage whites to hope that the end can be indefinitely postponed, particularly so if external economic pressure were to be relaxed.

Fear of the ultra-right has often been cited as a significant check on the government's freedom of action. So far as electoral considerations are concerned, the rival Conservative party may well be a decisive factor. But the neo-nazi Afrikaner Weerstandbeweging (AWB) represent a force that cannot be appeased and that could do a great deal of harm if its declared campaign of violence were allowed to gather strength. It is widely believed to have supporters within the police and armed forces, giving it access to intelligence and arms, and to the vast network of state terrorists maintained under previous governments, particularly under Botha's 'total strategy'. Yet, representing only a small minority of a minority, it could be more easily defeated than the anti-apartheid movement if the government were to act with resolution to disarm it and to purge the security forces of its partisans. That would be divisive and traumatic for Afrikaner nationalists, and might gain the Conservative party more votes, but it has been done before and is an indispensable condition of any peaceful transformation of power.

STATE INSTITUTIONS

So far we have considered the problem of democracy from the point of view of the prevailing attitudes and ideas among political groups and movements. It is, however, equally important to consider the state itself.

Democratic oppositions cannot achieve their aims without regard to the nature of the state under which they struggle. If the 'white democracy' is incapable of being simply expanded beyond racial bounds to embrace all South Africans, it is still crucial to know whether the state, itself, can be democratized: whether it can be adapted to function under democratic political conditions or (which is often mistaken for the same thing) can use or domesticate democracy. The answer may settle the issue of whether democracy in South Africa is, in an immediate sense, a necessarily revolutionary project, or whether it can issue from peaceful negotiation and accommodation (not only between races, but between state and people); whether, in other words, it necessitates a more or less violent rupture before, during, or after the transfer of power.

In many ways, it is a fundamental problem of democracy that, faced with *ancien régime* states which are refractory, it must to some considerable extent submit to a social and economic order of dominance, hostile to its purposes, but defended by the very state through which it must, somehow, seek to realize its aims. Democratic accession to power is barely a certain conquest, but is itself subject to the domination of the state. Democracy has, indeed, been put forward as an antidote to revolution, a strengthener of moderates among the disfranchised, a divider of the oppressed—as well as all the other good things that bear its name.

It would be idle to pretend that it could be otherwise. Democracy is inherently an accommodation among groups and classes with opposed interests and the way it manages those differences benefits some more than others. Though it may be hemmed in by a democratic constitution, the state itself is not a democratic thing. The essential question is that of its openness to the possibility of change this side of a leveling revolution. The answer varies from place to place and from age to age.

It is clear, nevertheless, that there must be some convergence between the state's needs and the masses' demand for enfranchisement. The state and the ruling class must, however reluctantly, come to see democracy or, at worst, the semblance of it, as an unavoidable part of the solution to a crisis they cannot otherwise resolve. Otherwise, the road to democracy is via civil war, or revolution.

If a democratic succession to apartheid arrives via a negotiated settlement, it is certain that the basic institutions of the state will survive the changeover, being reformed and adapted to the new political realities only afterward and by degrees. The existing bureaucracy which overrepresents Afrikaner nationalists, and reflects the apartheid hierarchy will take time to transform. Deracializing the public sector as a whole, including the management of major parastatals, will be a slow process. Until such state apparatuses are transformed, they may be expected to be potential sources of resistance to the new political order, and to the policies of any majority government.

The judiciary, which will be crucial to the interpretation of the democratic constitution and the maintenance of rights, is white, having faithfully served under the laws of apartheid despite the notable instances of independent rights-oriented thinking in recent years. The credibility of the judiciary, and popular acceptance of judicial decisions, will depend to a large extent on the degree to which the system will be seen to have changed.

But there is a more fundamental problem, namely, that of whether the judicial system can serve the purposes of a democratic constitutional order with the radical commitment to fundamental modification of existing economic and social relations: whether, with its present composition, training and traditions it will not become a bastion of conservatism rather than of reform and social transformation. Drastic reform of the judiciary itself could only be a gradual and cautious undertaking if democratic consensus is to be built up and maintained. The relationship between the courts and the governments of the day will affect, as it did under Nationalist party rule, the extent to which the state feels obliged to bypass judicial procedures and to resort to executive measures, and the degree of the electoral majority's support for such moves.

There is a hint in the behavior of elements of the judiciary in recent years that an institution originally 'packed' by the apartheid state, accustomed to affirming its impotence in the face of the executive and legislative power, may discover that its corporate and professional interests lie in adherence to universal notions of legality and judicial responsibility.

Much of the writing about 'the rule of law' in South Africa presupposes an objective law, neutral or indifferent to the major social struggles of the day, with the judges merely applying with professional detachment a body of clear law (or a Bill of Rights of uncontentious meaning). It is doubtful whether any democratic judicial system ever developed in this way. The maintenance of the rule of law depends on the credibility of the justice of the laws, and on the relations between the judicial system and the democratic consensus. Liberals predominantly focus on the threat to individual liberties which may arise from the way the majority government is likely to use state power. That, however, is a partial view and probably misses another important area of concern: that of the possible collusion of state structures including the judiciary with the political elites against popular interests; or, alternatively, the paralysis of a government that would be responsive to popular interests but which finds itself enclosed in a gilded cage by a recalcitrant state. The radical critique of judicial systems in Africa turns frequently on the conflict between social rather than individual interests with those of the state and the apparatus, like the judicial system, that serve it.

In a sense, the problem is one of determining how far a democratic system for South Africa would need to deviate from the idealized image of established democracies in order to meet the demands of its specific context, and how far it can differ and yet remain plausibly democratic. The matter turns on the degree of liberalism in liberal democracy: on how much of it is indispensable to democracy (given that an illiberal democracy would be nonsense), and how that portion might be realized, against an increasingly truculent, static view that democracy is either individualist and economic-liberal or it is not democracy at all.

The greatest problems of any successor government will be that of assimilating the security forces and integrating them in a new nonracial defense and security service alongside former guerrillas. There would be two immediate problems with the forces as presently constituted. First, they do provide a haven for profoundly antidemocratic elements that have distinguished themselves in repression at home, destablization abroad, and terrorism. More important, there is a real possibility that the military—Afrikaners and collaborating ethnic armies—could function as the armed wing of a losing political bloc constituted of the Nationalists (or some of them) and their former black collaborators. To neutralize them, or to persuade them to submit to democratic authority, would be no easy matter; to use them to quell a rightwing civilian revolt or secessionist rebellion would be extremely difficult.

While speculation abounds concerning the diversity of opinion among senior officers about the political future of the country, it is a fact that the military has in no way been prepared for the possibility of serving under an ANC government or with ANC officers. On the other hand, military service provides a living and a soldier needs an army. It is improbable that most officers would prefer the role of post-apartheid 'contras' except in circumstances where the 'white-black', 'left-right' compromise that produced a settlement had broken down among civilians. Similarly, the bulk of Afrikaner civil servants would have an obvious interest in accommodation than a civil war which they could not, eventually, win. The same must, eventually, apply to most military personnel. But there are powerful forces—of ideology, of ethnic solidarity, and of economic security—which will place limits on such pragmatism and it would be the task of good government to extend those limits while seeking to ensure that they are not exceeded. Nevertheless, every reform, every new departure, will be a potential constitutional crisis to be resolved on the way to democracy.

In principle, none of the problems of changing the apartheid character of the state is insuperable. Whether they are actually resolved will depend on events and situations that arise which are impossible to predict. There remains the problem, however, that the institutions might shed their attachment to the old order and yet be incapable of operating in the spirit of a democratic constitution. Peace in the state machinery, as in the economy and society generally, might well have to be purchased by a suppression of popular expectations which would also necessitate the nullification of democracy. The Latin American experience is a grim warning in this respect. Yet the instability of authoritarian dictatorships, and the continual reassertion popular interests through radical struggle, are also lessons of that experience, showing that even when eclipsed, the democratic ideal is not extinguished.

Might it not, then, eventually happen that the state and its apparatus, and therefore the fractions of classes most closely tied to them, come to find that they have no better hope of furthering their own interests than through democracy? Such a conversion would be conjunctural and not immutable, needing for a long time to be reinforced by the permanent contingency of popular struggle.

SOUTH AFRICA'S EXTERNAL RELATIONS

It would be a mistake to imagine that the democratization of South Africa is or can be a purely internal matter. Although this is not the appropriate place to discuss the matter at any length, it is as well to bear it in mind.

It was developments in external relations which were to accelerate the end of Botha's presidency and accelerate the movement towards a negotiated end of apartheid. Against the background of the campaign for international economic sanctions, South Africa's own setbacks in Angola—where Soviet assistance to the ruling MPLA against South African-backed UNITA rebels had been stepped up—and evidence of doubt among ordinary whites about the costs of this protracted war, Pretoria had begun to seek a negotiated end to its presence in Namibia and Angola. The decisive change in Soviet-United States relations progressively led the Soviet Union to seek a cooperative solution with the United States to Southern African problems and as much as possible seek to scale down its own commitments. Washington, for its part, under pressure of public and congressional opinion at home and seeing the Soviet threat to its interests in Southern Africa receding, became more accommodating to nationalist movements in the region, including the ANC—long held under suspicion because of its alliance with the South African Communist party. In the final months in office the Reagan administration speeded up the search for a solution to the problems of Namibian independence and the presence of Cuban troops in Angola which it had joined in its 'linkage politics'.[14] Sensing Washington's growing responsiveness, and under pressure from Moscow to be more conciliatory towards the West and towards whites in South Africa, the ANC adopted a posture of moderation and pragmatism, adding to Botha's dilemma. Pretoria could no longer make credible its identification of the anti-apartheid struggle with Soviet expansionism in Southern Africa, as it had done in various ways since 1948 when the National party first came to power. It became much easier for Pretoria's former anticommunist allies, who had all along been critical of its apartheid policies, to contemplate a new political order in South Africa and to support its emergence. The threat of economic sanctions became more real. That heightened the expectation of change within South Africa, and the belief grew among whites as well as blacks that negotiation between the government and the ANC, preceded by the release of Nelson Mandela and other political prisoners, had become inevitable. It was essentially, if indirectly, on this question that Botha fell out with his Cabinet and was forced to resign, paving the way for the accession of F.W. deKlerk who dramatically accelerated the movement toward a negotiated settlement in February 1990 by releasing Nelson Mandela and unbanning the proscribed African nationalist organizations and the Communist party.

South Africa has been a major subject of international interest for many years, and whether the campaign to secure trade sanctions to force a change in its governance succeeds or fails, its economic future depends on international acceptance of whatever solution it finds to its internal problems. In the present conjuncture with the revival of democratic movements in various parts of the world exciting considerable sympathy in like-minded countries—even at a time when the prevalent notions of democracy among major parties (in the Anglo-Saxon countries, at least) are narrower and less egalitarian than they have ever been since the war—it will be more difficult for Western states to be indifferent to the fate of democracy in South Africa.

International attention to the political resolution of regional conflicts tends to be highly dependent on events that capture the headlines and the focus of attention can shift capriciously from one trouble spot to the next. Southern Africa has been in danger of being overshadowed by Eastern Europe and the Arab World. The end of the Cold War, together with the apparent imminence of the end of apartheid, may greatly diminish external interest in the details of a political solution or the willingness to act to produce any particular kind of solution.

However, South Africa will continue to be of great economic interest to the major trading nations and to be influenced by their policies. The economic options available to any post-apartheid government will depend to a high degree on what foreign investors, bankers and intergovernmental agencies like the IMF and World Bank will accept. To a large extent, the option of large-scale nationalization is disqualified by the certain hostility it provokes in the West. Similarly, it may be expected that the need to maintain the confidence of the whites who dominate the economy, and to maintain a stable and profitable business environment, will place severe restraints on the kinds of state intervention to redress past wrongs. In a general way, the collapse of the Soviet system has all but excluded the option of a 'non-capitalist' path of development and many of the organizational and ideological alternatives it was supposed to provide.

This narrows the ground of possible ideological divergence between parties (which may be good for democracy); on the other hand, it constrains the range of action to correct radical inequalities and may create enormous problems of legitimation. Erstwhile radical liberation movements that can do no more than manage and reform piecemeal an economic order that many have sacrificed so much (as they believe) in order to *overthrow*, may provoke negative reactions of all kinds—

anomie and lawlessness, violent extremism, terrorism and a general cynicism corrosive of democracy.

There are neither the will nor the mechanisms to secure international action to forestall or arrest such a *dérapage*, not much grounds for hope for a radically different climate of international cooperation more helpful to egalitarian movements. What is certain is that while some of the old struggles may take new forms as a result of a transfer of power under a democratic constitution, they will nonetheless continue as before, against, both internal and international sources of oppression. And in South Africa, no less than in other states, they will test to the limit the possibility—and the possibilities—of democracy.

NOTES

1. For an earlier deal, see Nicholas Mansergh, *South Africa 1906-1961: The Price of Magnanimity*, New York: Praeger 1962.
2. See, among others, T. Lodge, *Black Politics in South Africa since 1945*, London: Longman, 1983; E. Roux, *Time Longer than Rope: A History of the Struggle of the Black Man for Freedom in South Africa*, Madison: Wisconsin University Press, 1964.
3. Some of these developments are usefully discussed in W.G. James ed., *The State of Apartheid*, Boulder Colorado, Lynne Rienner, 1987.
4. For wide-ranging discussion of the African transition from colonialism in its various aspects see, among others, P. Gifford and Wm. Roger Louis, *Decolonization and African Independence: The Transfers of Power 1960-1980*, New Haven: Yale University Press, 1988.
5. The conventional association of democracy with the rise of the bourgeoisie stresses the prosthetic aspect. Yet, it is possible to trace the roots of modern Western democracy back to aristocratic resistances to the consolidation of monarchial power even long before feudalism and,

indeed, subsequently, to feudal resistances to emergent sovereignty. In this case the conservative defense of privileges of 'rights' is the more important. Throughout this history, however, other classes and other strata had their own rights (stable expectations) and demands which had their effect.

6. Cf., No Sizwe, *One Azania, One Nation: The National Question in South Africa*, London: Zed Press, 1979 esp., 95-131.

7. A necessary process of ideological simplification which could clear the decks for a new appraisal of society—race and class—in the light of the political struggle.

8. See Tom Lodge, 'The United Democratic Front' in J. Brewster, ed., *Can South Africa Survive? Five Minutes to Midnight*, London: Macmillan 1980, 206-230.

9. See E. Webster, 'The Rise of Social-movement Unionism: The Two Faces of the Black Trade Union Movement in South Africa' in P. Frankel, N. Pines and M. Swilling, eds., *State, Resistance and Change in South Africa*, London: Croom Helm, 1988; also, P. van Niekerk, 'The Trade Union Movement in the Politics of Resistance in South Africa' in S. Johnson, ed., *South Africa: No Turning Back*, London: Macmillan, 1988.

10. The traditional preoccupations of South African Liberalism are sympathetically discussed in J. Butler and R. Elphick, *Democratic Liberalism in South Africa: Its History and Prospect*, Middletown, CT: Wesleyan University Press, 1987.

11. Among others, M. Murray, *South Africa: Time of Agony, Time of Destiny: The Upsurge of Popular Protest*, London: Verso, 1987; S. Johnson, "The Soldiers of Luthuli: Youth in the Politics of Resistance in South Africa", in S. Johnson, ed., *South Africa, No Turning Back* London: Macmillan 1988.

12. Such ideas had been debated for two decades or more, first in relation to the modification of the political status of Coloureds and later in the context of Botha's professed desire for reform. Some representative pieces may be found in D.J. van Vuuren and D. J. Kriek, *Political Alter-*

natives for Southern Africa: Principles and Perspectives, Durban: Butterworths, 1983.
13. This issue is dealt with more fully in my *The Constitutional Moment in South Africa* which is in preparation.
14. Cf., P.H. Baker: *The United States and South Africa: The Reagan Years,* New York: Ford Foundation, 1989.

CHAPTER 6

PROSPECTS OF LIBERAL DEMOCRACY IN SOUTH ASIA

Anirudha Gupta

South Asia is a repository of the world's poor. Over half of its 1.15 billion live in absolute poverty, another one-third without home or employment. Two out of every three adults are illiterate, 50 out of every 1,000 children die at birth and another 200 before they reach the age of five. In terms of per capita income (around $200) the region ranks below Latin America, West Asia and the Gulf.[1] These are somber facts, but the region also thrives on contrasts. Despite massive deprivation, great wealth has accumulated in a few hands, subsistence agriculture has produced islands of food surplus, festering slums in the cities have not checked the rise of luxury hotels, higher education has built a huge reservoir of trained manpower which seeks an outlet in the markets of West Asia and the Gulf, and science and technology have ridden on the back of bullock carts to lay the foundation of modern industries.

LIBERAL DEMOCRACY IN NON-WESTERN STATES

There are asymmetries too. With 72 percent of the area and 77 percent of the population, India leads the region in GNP, technology, armed forces, military expenditure, installed energy and world trade. Brazil is the only other comparable country in these terms but Brazil's ratios in respect to its neighbors are substantially lower than India's.[2] Size and power tend to go together, and within the subcontinent the government in New Delhi is very conscious of its dominance.

Among India's smaller neighbors, the nearest to measure up to its military strength is Pakistan, but its technoindustrial base remains very narrow. Sri Lanka, Bangladesh, Nepal, Bhutan and Maldives have no industrial capacity worth the name. They depend entirely on the export of primary goods and are extremely vulnerable to the vagaries of the world market: they also require foreign aid and investment on a much larger scale than does India; hence the numerical weakness of an indigenous entrepreneur class in these countries. In contrast, India's big industrial houses operate through regional enterprises and provide a livelihood to a huge body of educated manpower. To borrow a Marxist phrase, the Indian bourgeoisie has found a socioeconomic base which is absent elsewhere in South Asia.

Does this contribute to India's political stability and democratic structure? It must, for without a social base to support political stability, democratic institutions can hardly function. This is one commodity India's neighbors eminently lack. Since its inception, Pakistan has gone through three military phases until the elections of 1988 partially handed power to an elected civilian government. In East Pakistan, which became the sovereign republic of Bangladesh in 1971, two civilian heads of government and state were assassinated (Sheikh Mujib in 1975 and Zia-ur-Rahman in 1981) before the military took control—for a second time—under General H.M. Ershad. Civilian rule returned early in 1990 but the army waits in the wings. In Sri Lanka a democratic system survived a Marxist insurrection in 1971 only to find itself caught by an all-out civil war between the Sinhala and Tamil communities. Even the Maldives, with 1200 coral islands and a population of 181,500, witnessed a "pocket coup" which was dramatically stamped out by a force of India paratroopers in November 1988. Only in Nepal and Bhutan—the two tiny Himalayan kingdoms—has political order been preserved in the hands of traditional monarchies, but they too face popular stirrings in favor of democratization. In Nepal, the King granted universal adult franchise in 1979 to broaden the base of the Panchayat system; a decade of political uncertainty followed until the appointment of a democratic government led by the Nepal Congress party in April 1990. The Bhutanese monarch coopted powerful elite families to preempt any sudden challenge on his authority but events in Nepal had their effect on the government in Thimphu.

India, too, has had its share of acute political crisis. It has not so far faced any military challenge to civilian authorities, but it did pass through a period of internal emergency (1975-1977) when all opposition parties and expressions of political dissent were banned. At times, regional and ethnic protests in Punjab, caste unrest in Bihar and tribal violence in Assam and the northeast have turned Delhi into an "imperial city" under siege; yet, with the exception of Kashmir and Punjab (where language and religion provide grist to secessionist movements), violence has underlined the desire of different communities(tribes, castes and regions) to redefine their places *within* the Indian union. To the extent that these desires are part of a democratic bargain, they make the Indian federal system more flexible. In this respect, the reification of the Indian state has been a remarkable product of its social and economic turmoil.

This assertion of a strong centralized rule is not peculiar to India. It is also a feature of its smaller neighbors. Except for Bangladesh, which emerged as a result of an internecine war within undivided Pakistan, no regional or secessionist movement has gained recognition as an independent state. Even in

Sri Lanka, the Jaffna Tamil rebels have seemingly abandoned their struggle for a breakaway "Eelam."[3] One reason why the state has been able to weather the storm of political violence is "the excessive enlargement of power control and regulation it has come to enjoy in most Third World countries."[4] The explanation (says Hamza Alavi) lies in the primacy of the state above contending classes and movements, a trend further helped by the belief that the state has a special relationship to the public good. In an economically backward and socially unequal society, the state must play an interventionist role, especially in the economy, which gives rise to the phenomenon of "command politics."[5] In a sense, the traditional liberal concept of the state as a third actor is replaced by the concept of state as a central actor in society. "In this reading, the state not only provides order, justice, and security, enhances social goods and benefits, and reduces or eliminates social costs, but it also directly commands enough resources to be self-determining in a variety of policy areas and historical contexts."[6]

Such arguments raise an interesting issue, *viz*, under what circumstances will the state—which claims to be the means of solving problems and achieving goals—itself become the problem? The issue gains importance because the prospects of liberal democracy can be assessed only in the context of an over-powerful and over-centralized state in the fragmented national societies of South Asia, taking us beyond the confines of regimes which are civilian or military, democratic or authoritarian. State power in India based on the ballot box can be as distant and arbitrary in its use of patronage and coercion as in any nondemocratic polity. The difference is that, whereas the rulers of nondemocracies are insecure because they lack any popular mandate to legitimize authority, democratic rulers face no such problems. Indeed, it is precisely because they are elected that they justify themselves when interfering with the judiciary or with civil rights and parliamentary procedures. Despite India's democratic path, the government imposed a two-year ban on all opposition parties. Similarly, Sri Lanka's presidential system (1978) reduced the elected parliament to "an appendage of the executive."[7]

This poses a further set of questions. If a democratic system fails to check the over-centralization of executive power, as in Sri Lanka and India, what measures can be taken to deter the exercise of such powers? Put this way, the question assumes that in a democracy, arbitrary behavior of the executive is a temporary phenomenon, but in the non-democracies—Pakistan, Bangladesh, Nepal, Bhutan—the issue has been not only one of finding correctives but of ensuring popular freedom *vis-á-vis* repressive governments. It is interesting in this connection to note that no military regime has considered itself to be a permanent solution to Pakistan's problems. Both Ayub Khan (1958-1969) and Yahya Khan (1969-1972) initiated reforms to hand political power to the duly elected civilian governments. President Zia-ul-Huq's rule(1977-1987) had the distinction of being the "first unmitigated military regime in Pakistan," but it too finally bowed to pressure to grant limited freedom to civilian parties. In Bangladesh, General Ershad was forced out of office by his political opponents who demanded an elected government. Similarly in Nepal, the king of Nepal was obliged to move not only towards an adult franchise but a part-controlled government.[8]

Despite their outward show of strength, therefore, the nondemocratic regimes in South Asia face what can be described as 'the threat of democratization'. In India and Sri Lanka, on the other hand, the operation of democratic institutions has posed new problems. When in Sri Lanka, the major parties replaced each other turn and turn about by outbidding for majority Sinhalese support, the effect was to marginalize minority Tamils. The latter resorted to violence not to try and secure a more prominent place within the Sri Lankan polity but for an independent Tamil state (Eelem). This, in turn, invited greater use of counterviolence by the Sri Lankan government. An apparently successful democratic regime thus fell back on military means to secure its own survival. Why did this happen? Did the transplant of the Western model of democratic majority rule in an ethnically divided society give rise to the government's militarization of its rule?

India traversed a different path. Under its 1950 constitution, the country became a secular, democratic state with particular emphasis on the rights and protection of minority and backward communities. Accepting these principles, Indian political parties (barring a few ultra Left and Right groups) joined the electoral fray. Being in government at independence and having an all-India organizational base, the Congress party was able to project itself as the sole protector of the weaker section. In a social setting of great inequalities, Congress found it easy to turn these weaker communities into safe "vote-banks." But there was always the persistent belief that, for its own survival, Congress needed these divisions based on caste, religion and economic deprivation. After all, the promise of "Garibi Hatao" ('remove poverty') would make no sense if the mass of the electorate were not poor. Moreover, competition on party lines, on the familiar Western model, kept alive fragmentation of Indian society by feeding on its own divisions.

We can broadly summarize our formulations: (a) societies in South Asia are overburdened by massive poverty, under-nourishment, and illiteracy; (b) in economic terms the distance between the rich and the poor remains unbridgeable; (c) this has not given rise to class conflict of the type familiar in the Western societies: the state with its powers of coercion and patronage has attained an autonomous status over all classes; (d) for security reasons and domestic compulsions, the state has grown stronger, all the more so because of its interventionist role in economic and other spheres; (e) countries under military-bureaucratic or monarchical regimes face a groundswell of demands for political liberalization; for example, elected legislatures, an independent judiciary, universal franchise, etcetera; and (f) in countries with democratic institutions but with deep social fractures an elected government may act in a manner which nullifies the very objectives of democratic liberalism. In Sri Lanka, majoritarian politics led to the marginalization of the minority; in India, social and economic inequalities have become the *raison d'être* of party politics.

So much by way of general introduction. We turn now to three specific areas of inquiry. First, the factors which influenced the development of democratic institutions in India and Sri Lanka. Second, the character of the nondemocratic system of the region. Third, the future shape of politics in South Asia.

INDIA AND SRI LANKA: DIVERGENT EXPERIENCE

British withdrawal from the subcontinent in 1947-1948 followed the installation of parliamentary government in India and Sri Lanka. Prime Minister Jawaharlal Nehru's personal authority and his hold on the Congress party were central to the establishment of the primacy of the prime minister's office and confirmation of the role of the president as a nominal head of state. Although the relationship between the prime minister and president has been occasionally soured, the validity of India's cabinet system based on the British model has never been seriously questioned.[10]

The parliamentary system in Sri Lanka, on the other hand, underwent a radical change with the adoption of a de Gaulle-type presidential system in 1978. The change was made possible because of the overwhelming majority (83.3 percent) which the ruling United National party enjoyed in parliament. The new system was justified on the ground that "speedy implementation of development politics could be realized in such a system, because the president would not be subject to the 'constituency' considerations that legislators were."[11] Yet until 1978, the running of democratic institutions in India and Sri Lanka were strikingly similar. Both countries held regular parliamentary elections (in India also at the state level). Voting percentage averaged 60 percent although, in the Sri Lankan elections of 1970 and 1977, polling was more than 85 percent. Since election results were determined on the basis of a single-majority constituency,[12] large parties with organized political structures gained more seats than their share of votes warranted. In India, the Congress party held sway at the center except in 1977 and 1989 when the Opposition was able to engage in a straight contest against Congress at national level. But whereas the experience of India has generally been one of Congress dominance, in Sri Lanka political power has oscillated between the major Sinhala parties—UNP and SLPP. Yet in both countries, governments were formed by parties which never polled more than 40 percent of the votes (see Appendix II). Only in 1977 did the UNP secure more than 50 percent of the vote when it secured 83 percent of the seats in Parliament. In India the Congress share of votes prior to its defeat in 1989, was usually below 50 per cent despite its comfortable majority of seats in parliament. By contrast, the party's share of votes in state elections has rarely been below 40 per cent, yet it failed to form governments at state level where opposition parties were able to pool votes and defeat the Congress.

INDIA

The long absence of an all-India alterative to Congress until the late 1980s accounted for a number of peculiarities in India's political system. First, the threat that the Opposition might combine (as in 1977 and 1989) and put it out of office led the Congress to adopt three broad strategies: (a) keep the Opposition divided by inducements or other means; (b) obstruct the opposition-run state governments through central agencies of the administration in Delhi, including use of the office of state governor; and (c) populist rhetoric and patronage to win over disgruntled elements in such states. None of these, however, could ensure the loyalty of Congress in times of leadership crisis. Hence, the second feature, namely, a transformation of the ruling party into a highly centralized organization under the prime minister's autocratic control—Jawaharlal Nehru, Mrs. Gandhi and Rajiv Gandhi. In the process Congress came to resemble "more a state-dominated party lacking any autonomous institutional authority of its own. The old system of the Congress party, which had encouraged regional and local leaders to build sustained social bases of support, is now perceived as a threat to the plebiscitarian organization. The old idea of a party-based state was transformed into a state-based party."[17]

One result of this transformation was the decline of Congress, and the growth in number and strength of its opponents, some regionally based, others appealing to religious sentiment. Unable or unwilling to meet such challenges by a reform of the party's own democratic structures, the government of Mrs. Gandhi used emergency powers. The 59th Amendment of the Constitution, along with other ordinances, empowered the state to arrest, detain and punish any person on grounds of public security without due process of law. The *Economic and Political Weekly* commented on the government's reaction to those who opposed it:

> The recent terrorist and disruptive activities do away with rights afforded to citizens either constitutionally or through acts of parliament. Moreover, they are contrary to important principles enshrined in the International Covenant of Civil and Political Rights to which India is a party.[13]

Mrs. Gandhi was defeated in 1977. She returned to office three years later but was assassinated by members of her Sikh bodyguard in October 1984. Rajiv Gandhi trod the same path. At first acclaimed, and elected in December 1984 in a landslide victory, he and Congress went down to defeat in 1989 at the hands of a loose alliance of center, Left and Right parties amidst accusation of corruption and autocracy.[14] The attack was directed by V.P. Singh (a former congress finance minister) and his Janata Dal party; the Left was based on the communist vote in Bengal; the rightwing Bhariya Janata party raised the saffron flag of Hindu belief across the northern Hindu-speaking states.

Uncertainty bred confusion. Within a year of taking office, V.P. Singh was replaced by Chandra Shekhar whose breakaway Janata Dal group was supported in parliament by Congress. Then a further contest early in 1991—India's tenth general election since independence—brought the terrible death of Rajiv Gandhi in a bomb explosion during a party rally at Sriperumbudur near Madras. Voting was interrupted, but not cancelled, and it ended with Congress once more in office, although without a majority of seats in the new parliament.[15] There were now two unfamiliar features. The prime minister is a Congress stalwart, P.V. Narasimha Rao, but not a member of the Nehru-Gandhi dynasty; and he is from the southern state of Andhra Pradesh.

The picture today is confused. The BJP now has a strong northern base. It gives a voice and a political presence to Hindu sentiments that will not easily be muffled. But the return of Congress, under a new leader on a middle ground of support between opposed groups, may actually have strengthened the prospects of renewed democratic government. As Amulya Ganguli noted in *The Statesman* on June 12, 1991, "the two major obstacles which had kept the Congress (I) distinct from other parties—its preeminence and its dynastic preferences—have disappeared. It is now a 'normal party' which may be more easily incorporated into a democratic framework of politics."

The growth of regional unrest may also be more complicated and, therefore, less serious than might at first be thought. Kashmir apart, unrest mirrors specific grievances of particular communities many of whose leaders seek justice *within* the framework of Indian federalism. The violence which disfigures political life is horrifying, but it is also internally destructive—Sikh against Sikh, Assamese against Assamese—when those who demand secession or separate statehood are opposed within their own community. Moreover, the genesis of a particular agitation often starts a new cycle of conflict within a state or region. Concessions to the linguistic grievances of the Assamese inspired a powerful movement among the Bodo tradesmen. In Andhra Pradesh, the Telegu Desam has faced a deluge of counterclaims from rival groups. Even within Punjab, Sikhs have been the worst sufferers from Sikh demands for Khalistan. Conflict thus shifts from a center-state axis to the subregions and community factions within a state. And such quarrels afford the central government every opportunity for maneuver.

Against such hopes for democracy and of unity, one must acknowledge a fear, not that dissent will fracture the state, but that the state may turn too readily to repression. Political violence in Kashmir and Punjab has been kept under control by an army and police administration, and the impact of the state's counterterror policies invests the executive with an immense range of powers unrelated to legislative scrutiny in a parliamentary system. Democracy by force of argument (to paraphrase a Bangladeshi scholar) may give place to democracy by the argument of force.[16] The threat in India might then come not from the formal abandonment of democratic institutions but their marginalization.

Does the fear reflect simply the failings of past leaders? Or is it more deep-seated?[17] One cannot be sure. India's political system has thrown up issues which are not familiar to the practice of Western democracies, but to conclude from this that democracy is a non-western society is unworkable or aberrant would make a mockery of the universal appeal of democratic issues.

SRI LANKA

Sri Lanka differs from India in one important respect: its western educated elite, which took over power at independence, had no experience of working with the commoners. If anything, its members had a profound contempt for the kind of mass agitation which the Indian congress organized during the nationalist period. If the business of running governments is best left to an educated elite—highly proficient in administration—on a formal grant of adult franchise, then it must be said that these conditions were fully met by the (Donoughmore) reforms of 1931. Indeed, it was the success of Sri Lanka's parliamentary committee system which prompted the British to grant political independence to the island on the strength of three premises:

1. an indigenous elite with high administration skills could steer the course of Westminster democracy in a non-western society;

2. such an elite would assist democracy in a non-western society;

3. a unitary system was essential for the national integrity of Sri Lanka.[18] For awhile the system worked. But unlike the committee regime (1931-1948) which limited the scope of party politics, the independence constitution provided for a cabinet system based on whichever party won a majority of seats in parliamentary elections. This threw open the gate for mass participation in the functioning of representative government. But in a society where the distance between governing and nongoverning classes had hitherto gone challenged, party competition led to an unprecedented upsurge of political demands among the Sinhalese majority. The rarefied structure of elite-run administration collapsed under the combined impact of Buddhist revivalism, a Sinhala language movement *(Swabhasa)* and widespread unrest among the semieducated unemployed and a poorly rewarded peasantry. For awhile, social disorder threatened to unleash the forces of political anarchy, but parliamentary democracy survived because S.W.R. Bandaranaike, the founder of the Sri Lanka Freedom party, was able to harness many of these disparate elements to a broad coalition called Mahajan Eksath Paramuna (MEP). The coalitions' victory in the 1956 elections induced illiterate peasant masses into a participatory democ-

racy but by its emphasis on Sinhala culture, religion and language it also changed the complexion of Sri Lankan politics. In effect, rule by majority was synchronized with the rule of the majority community. In subsequent years, the Bandaranaike government took several measures—such as the official language act, the standardization of higher education, restrictions on the employment of Tamils in the public services and large-scale Sinhala colonization of the Eastern province—each of which contributed to the ethnic negation of Sri Lankan Tamils.[19] The present roots of Sinhala-Tamil conflict can be traced to the watershed year of 1956.

What we see is interesting. The democratic system was able to absorb the stresses of social revolution (albeit on the political plane) but at a price *viz*, making the two major parties—UNP and SLPP—prisoners of Sinhala majoritarian demands. Whereas India's secular (noncommunal) stance ensured autonomy of the political leadership *vis-á-vis* the Hindu majority, in Sri Lanka the leadership succumbed wholesale to majority pressure. When it tried to resist, the result was disastrous: Bandaranaike's effort to accommodate Tamil grievances led to his assassination by a Buddhist monk (1959). When President Jayewardene (UNP) discussed the possibility of a limited devolution to the Tamil community, he not only whetted the appetite of Tamil separatists but gave a new lease of life to the extremist Sinhalese JVP (Janatha Vimukthi Peramuna).

A measure of populism is always inherent in such a situation. Following her husband's assassination Mrs. Bandaranaike promised to build a socialist society. The pledge swept the SLFP to power with a two-thirds majority (see Appendix III), enabling her government not only to pass a series of laws nationalizing foreign-owned concerns but, at the same time, giving Buddhism the foremost place in a new constitution (1972). "Socialist" control of the economy vastly expanded the bureaucratic apparatus operating behind "an institutional edifice of a centralized democracy" which lacked any functional equilibrium between the legislature, executive and judiciary.[20]

Economic failure and empty socialist slogans led to great public disenchantment within the Sinhalese electorate. Fresh elections in 1977 brought in a massive UNP majority in parliament. The economy was thrown open to free enterprise and foreign investment, but the centralization of executive powers was further consolidated with the promulgation of a presidential constitution. Presidential discretion was put outside judicial review, and a controversial referendum (1982) allowed Jayewardene to extend his tenure of government by a further five years.

President Jayewardene was more inclined perhaps than other leaders to concede autonomy to the Tamil minority in spheres of language and education, but the Tamils were now in no mood to accept limited concessions. Abandoning earlier federal claims, a younger more violent element turned to revolutionary demands for a separate Tamil state. At this point an extraneous factor became apparent. The Indian government was accused of giving large-scale military assistance to, and training a number of, Tamil groups not only in Jaffna but in Madras. With a huge Tamil population across the Palk straits in Tamil Nadu, the Sinhalese have never been free from the fear of being reduced to a minority in their own land. As casualties grew in the savage guerilla warfare between the Sri Lankan army and Tamil Tigers in the Jaffna Peninsula, Indian troops landed in the north following an accord between Indian Prime Minister Rajiv Gandhi and Jayewardene in July 1987.[21] The Indian Peace Keeping Force (IPKF) was then caught up in its own fierce conflict with the largest Tamil militant group—the Liberation Tigers of Tamil Eelan (LTTE). Prolongation of the conflict produced a chauvinist backlash in the south of the island. JVP (Sinhalese) violence spread like a forest fire which neither Jayewardene nor his successor, President Premedasa, was able to put out until quenched by the counterterror of government forces and local vigilantes.

PAKISTAN: GROPING FOR A POLITICAL ORDER

Liberal democracy was never given a chance in Pakistan. This was so, not because Pakistan had an "antidemocratic culture,"[22] but because of the circumstances of its birth. Its founder, Muhammad Ali Jinnah, did not conceive a separate Islamic state in the way it came to him. His dispute with the Congress leaders was over the future of the Muslim community in a free India. Congress claimed that it represented all classes and communities and, therefore, Muslims had nothing to fear from a Congress-dominated government. The Muslim League rejected this, and pressed for exclusive representation of Muslims in a future political dispensation. This was the "two-nation" theory on the basis of which the subcontinent was partitioned; but instead of incorporating all Muslims, Pakistan represented a union of two Muslim-majority territories—geographically removed from each other by a thousand miles. The arrangement worked fitfully until 1971 when the East broke away to become the independent republic of Bangladesh.

This event, in retrospect, showed that whatever might have been its original attraction, Islamic faith alone was not sufficient to hold a nation-state together. Two other factors were equally important: (a) Pakistan's immense regional and ethnic diversities, and (b) the ambiguities of its rulers towards the building of a theocratic state. Both require some elaboration.

At its birth Pakistan contained a number of mutually exclusive linguistic and ethnic groups: Punjabis with 60 percent of the population of West Pakistan, followed by Sindhis, Pathans and Baluch tribals; the Bengali of East Pakistan had accounted for over 50 percent of the population of undivided Pakistan. There were also divergent socioeconomic patterns: Punjab was under a powerful landowning aristocracy which supplied a high proportion of the officers corps of the Pakistan army; Sindh had a well-organized commercial class; the Bengali comprised generally a mass of poor peasants, while the Pathans and Balochs were tough tribesmen. There was also the ill-assorted milieu that made up the bulk of Muslim League supporters, mainly immigrants from the former United Provinces. As immigrants (*Mujaheer*) from India, they failed to win support from any of the entrenched ethnic groups. The Sindhis objected to *Mujaheer* domination of Karachi; the Punjabi landlords were opposed to the League's political leadership, and Muslims in East Pakistan, NWFP and Baluchistan interpreted the League's rule as an effort to impose *Mujaheer* primacy.[23]

The western-educated Muslim League leaders, who created Pakistan, were also not disposed to concede a large political role to the clergy. For the League, Islam was a political, not a religious, slogan and Jinnah made it clear that he was not willing to lead a theocratic state.[24] But the equation between religion and state was by no means clear. Pakistan's rulers used religion for purposes of consolidating the unity of the new state and to this end they compromised with the fundamentalists from time to time in symbolic gesture. Thus, Zulfikar Ali Bhutto called his ideology "Islamic Socialism," and Zia boldly promulgated the "Islamization" of the judicial system.[25]

After the demise of Jinnah and Liaqat Ali Khan, the League dissembled in the face of numerous parties and groups clamoring for a decisive role in Islamic Pakistan and such fractionalized politics persisted throughout the formative years (1951-1958). Somewhat surprisingly, the venality of the politicians in the quarrels among themselves did not diminish their formal commitment to democracy. The 1956 constitution which they produced was "almost classically democratic, providing for broad freedom of the people, political organizations, and the press, a responsible parliamentary system, and a federal structure that allocated responsibility to the elites of the subjects that were most crucial to them."[26]

But the survival of democracy was also related to Pakistan's obsession *vis-à-vis* India. The three Indo-Pak wars (1948, 1965 and 1971) aggravated this obsession, and the combination of external fears and political instability opened the way for military intervention. In 1958, General Ayub Khan proclaimed martial law, banned all political parties and abolished the 1956 constitution.

The military spelled out three basic priorities for Pakistan; (a) a strictly centralized state with little autonomy for the provinces; (b) immense expansion of the military-bureaucratic apparatus—especially for security purposes; and (c) preservation of Punjab's landowning classes. The soldier politicians were by no means unsuccessful. Impressive economic growth was registered during the two long spells of military rule (Ayub Khan 1958-1969 and the Zia period 1977-1987), then free play was given to market law and foreign collaboration. Substantial shifts in population and employment also gave rise to new industrialists, small-scale entrepreneur and a growing industrial working class. But the biggest gainer was the military as Pakistan forged strategic links with the United States during the latter's obsession with the Soviet Union and after the Soviet invasion of Afghanistan in 1980.

Occasionally, the organized interests of the armed forces clashed with the political program of the rulers. Yet except for the initial phase of Zia's rule, no army regime offered an alternative to a civilian-run political order. Paradoxically, the three factors mentioned above—stability, security and unity—put a limit to military authoritarianism. The two wars with India in 1965 and 1971 were regarded as a blow to Pakistan's national security. Hence, both Ayub and Yahya Khan had to quit office in humiliating circumstances. The myth of a united Pakistan collapsed with the army's failure to put down unrest in the East Wing, while the links of army officers with the landowning families of Punjab obstructed the process of socioeconomic reforms. Punjabi domination of politics, on the other hand, gave rise to strong centrifugal forces, and the repressive methods used in Sindh in 1983 fanned ethnic unrest in other parts. Unlike India, regionalism in Pakistan became wholly anticenter and, therefore, less amenable to political readjustment.

Any step towards democratization in Pakistan, therefore, has to be viewed in the context of several sensitivities: first, the army's own sectarian interests; second, the demands of the ethnic and linguistic groups; third, the economic thrusts of the Punjabi landowning classes; and fourth, sensitivity in regard to Pakistan's territorial integrity. Taken together, they constitute a formidable combination of interests and sensibilities for any government to meet in any part of the world.

BANGLADESH: AN EXERCISE IN ESCAPISM

In undivided Pakistan, the East Wing complained of economic exploitation and non-representation of the Bengali in the army and bureaucracy. But its crucial grievance centered on linguistic-cultural issues. In the 1950s the Bengali resisted the imposition of Urdhu. In the late 1960s, the urban-based intelligentsia and students launched a popular agitation against the Western wing. Matters came to a head when Sheikh Mujibur Rahman's Awami League was prevented from forming a civilian government in spite of the majority of seats it secured in the 1970 elections.[27] It provoked a violent mass upheaval and an equally violent reaction on the part of Islamabad which turned to the military. The result was a huge breakdown of law and order, and finally Indian military intervention in the civil war. Such was the birth of Bangladesh in 1971.

Mujibur Rahman's Awami League government (1971-1985) was then accused of leaning too much on Indian support, an affront to the newly asserted nationalism of the Bengali intelligentsia. Anti-Mujibur factions, in league with the roaming bands of the Mukti Bahini who had stored plentiful supplies of arms and ammunition during the civil war, soon created a high level of disorder. In addition, allegations of corruption and inefficiency rocked the government. For a time Mujib tried to save face by imposing one-party rule under a presidential system; but the experiment was cut short with the assassination of Mujib and members of his family by a group of army officers in August 1975.

Unlike Pakistan, Bangladesh did not have to confront ethnic opposition (except from a handful of *Ghakmas* in Chittagong district) but other factors intervened. There was the students' traditional opposition to authority, the impoverization of the peasantry and, the activities of numerous factions within the army and administration. All this forced the military rulers to invent civilian allies: Major General Ziaur Rahman floated his own political party (Bangladesh National Party) to win the Presidential elections of 1978.[28] When in 1986 General Ershad gave way to political pressures to hold elections on the basis of a new constitution, his supporters organized a new party (Jatiya Dal) which faced opposition from two rival coalitions. One was under the Awami League led by Mujibur Rahman's daughter (Sh Hasina), the other (the BNP) under the leadership of Zia's widow (Begum Zia). Despite a very low turnout, and the BNP's sudden withdrawal, the elections gave Jatiya Dal a large majority. Ershad formed a new government and began what he described as the "transition to democracy." In August, he resigned as army chief of staff to announce his candidacy for the presidency and was elected in October with nearly 22 million votes (his nearest rival receiving 1.5 million votes in an official turnout of 54 percent voters).

The Bangladesh experience belies the hope that a culturally homogeneous society, bound by language and religion, can readily build a liberal democracy. Political fragmentation is perhaps a phenomenon of poor societies when poverty itself poses an obstacle to the promotion of liberal institutions. What kind of system can one expect in a country which, afflicted by natural disasters, also has 30 million landless, 15 million unemployed and 0.6 million educated unemployed? Can any government meet even the basic human needs of such a society?

NEPAL AND BHUTAN: TRADITIONAL MONARCHIES

Although both Bhutan and Nepal are monarchies, their political evolution differs greatly. Bhutan follows a policy of positive isolation, and strict immigration laws have so far kept intact its traditional way of life centered on the Buddhist church and the crown. To win over the loyalty of chiefly families, the king has set up a partially elected assembly (*Tshogdu*) and a royal advisory council (*Lodoi Tshokde*).[30] The kingdom also gives limited guarantees to Nepali immigrants—easy acceptance as citizens, employment and promotion in state services—and these help to preserve a traditional autocratic order despite "pro-democracy riots" in the southern part of the kingdom towards the end of 1970.

In 1950, the Rana oligarchy which had kept the Nepali monarch out of public affairs suddenly caved in under the combined pressure of an anti-Rana movement organized by the Nepali Congress, the sudden flight of King Tribhuvan to Delhi, and India's direct intervention on behalf of the King. In 1951, a coalition ministry of Rana and Nepali Congress representatives was formed under the general guidance of King Tribhuvan. The period that followed (1951-1959) witnessed the making and unmaking of several short-lived ministries and fragmentation in the ranks of the Ranas and the Nepali Congress, both of which helped the political ascendancy of the king.[31] Nevertheless, a more liberal constitution was adopted to provide a form of cabinet government, and elections were held in 1959 which gave B.P. Koirala's National Congress 74 of the 123 seats in the national assembly. In December 1960, however, King Mahendra dismissed the Koirala ministry, dissolved parliament, banned all political parties and established his own version of royal authoritarianism. This consisted of a nominated *Panchayat* (assembly) and a group of advisors (council of ministers). The king used the frailty of local politicians to win over 60 percent of the former members of the Nepali Congress to run the new system. But politics by control has its own contradictions: factions emerged within the Panchayat, politicians intimidated each other in the name of the king, and students in Kathmandu took to the streets to call for an end to the system. This unnerved the new monarch, King Birendra. A referendum to find out if his people were in favor of an improved constitution based on adult franchise provided for a straight contest between supporters and opponents of the Panchayat system. The former won by a narrow majority but, sensing rightly that his subjects wanted change, the king granted free elections for a parliament without political parties. In 1981, and again in 1986, elections were fought by candidates on a non-party basis.

The turning point came at the end of the 1980s and early 1990s when prodemocracy strikes by lawyers, doctors and airline pilots evoked a mass demonstration against the palace and a violent government response by the army. The result was that in April 1990 King Birenda accepted a multiparty government headed by K.P. Bhattarai of the Nepali Congress party, plus the communist controlled United Left Front. The 1962 Panchyat constitution was abolished and replaced by an elected House of Assembly.

The long years of Panchayat administration witnessed vast changes in Nepal's socioeconomic life. The feudal structure of political authority has given place to a centrally organized administrative system, the influx of foreign aid and expatriates has speeded up developmental programs. On average, 186 km of road have been built each year since 1956, an improvement in transport and communication which has facilitated administrative integration. The average life expectancy of the Nepalese has gone up, as has the literacy rate. In education, the number of students enrolled in secondary and high education between 1950 and 1970 rose from 2,000 to 120,000 which, together with the expansion of administrative and social services, accounted for the emergence of a sizeable middle class.[32]

PROSPECTS

Certain general observations follow:

1. Notwithstanding the inequalities and divisions within these South Asian societies, there is an undeniable pressure on their rulers to broaden the arena of political participation. This is apparent not only in India and Sri Lanka but in countries where as-yet democratic institutions are weak or absent. If voters' choice in controlled or partyless elections can be an indicator, then slight shifts towards democratization cannot be denied in the case of Bhutan and Pakistan. More than 60 percent of the registered voters in Nepal participated in the last two elections: in Pakistan's parliamentary elections (November 1988) the polling percentage was 54 percent. Even in Bangladesh, some polling took place in the 1986 elections. In Sri Lanka, the average turnout of voters in the 1988-1989 presidential and parliamentary elections was below 60 percent and that was certainly a great fall from the 87 percent voting of 1970,[33] a fall accounted for by the outbreak of widespread violence and disorder in the island. Yet even this lower percentage underscored a "tradition of participating in elections and changing governments in our political culture.... Despite the violent campaign that sought to undermine the electoral process, people did come out and vote."[34]

2. One may ask, "what can a large turnout of poor and illiterate voters indicate? Do not such voters become easy victims of electoral manipulation?" This is true, but only partly. The Indian electorate was systematically intimidated during the emergency years of 1975-1977 but Mrs. Gandhi went down to defeat. The same, perhaps, holds true about Mrs. Bandaranaike's defeat in the Sri Lankan elections in the same year. Her "socialist measures" had succeeded in driving out essential goods from the market while swelling the ranks of her detractors. Hence, the UNP was returned with an absolute majority of the votes cast.

3. In both India and Sri Lanka elected governments, with a minority of votes, have taken advantage of the state's vast

resources to wield increasingly authoritarian powers. In India, it became a general tendency under the party dominance of the Congress. The routine operation of democratic institutions such as an adult franchise, elected legislatures, a free press and representation of the backward communities in government failed to check the state's arbitrary use of power. As the Rudolphs point out, "(in India) the self-determining state is in a position to serve itself and, like other self-interested actors, to be a source of exploitation or injustice."[35] This raises the unresolved theme of state authority versus popular sovereignty that philosophers have debated since the days of Plato.

4. The issue gets further complicated in view of the rich and poor divide in non-Western societies. Helplessness on the part of the poor to fight social and economic inequalities encourages a concentration of power and resources in the hands of a privileged few with the result that, even when the state enunciates an ideology of social justice, its results are disappointing. In such societies, competition for political power contrives to perpetuate old inequalities in a new garb. All political parties in India have perfected the art of keeping alive the sectional interests of the minorities, backward classes, and the tribals in order to win their support during the elections. In the process, what we have are the "vote banks"—as noted above. What solution can liberal democracy offer to correct the situation? It is impossible for India's political parties to make good the promises they make to the voters. On the other hand, the hope of a paradise of plenty (*Ram Rajya*) makes sense to those who live in absolute scarcity, and an egalitarian rhetoric prospers best when escape from inequality is impossible.

5. In India's federal system, an over-centralization of power by the center has weakened the hold of the ruling Congress party in the states. The trend has given rise to several regional forces which must be met either with force or with concessions to avoid a serious threat to national integrity. The danger is that of an increased use of the military to assert the center's

authority at the regional level. In Sri Lanka an accretion of the executive's power provoked so great a cycle of violence and counterviolence that it nearly dismantled the unity and integrity of the nation-state.[36] In Pakistan too, recurrent secessionist demands against a Punjabi-dominated center led the military to remove Benazir Bhutto's civilian government in August 1990 under a presidential decree.

6. Another related factor is the transformation of South Asian societies under the impact of technology, education and new means of production. The dynamics of social change are visible everywhere, though not uniformly in all parts of the region. In Bhutan the feudal order survives, although under growing stress; Nepal, on the other hand, has seen the rise of a new middle class which is extremely articulate in defending the kingdom's nationhood. India's agrarian society, too, is fast changing. In place of quasi-feudal relations, a new class of small to medium sized, self-employed, agricultural producers, called the "bullock capitalists," has emerged. They represent a new force which no party, including those on the Left, has been able to ignore; but the individualistic character of the 'bullock capitalist class' makes it an agent of resistance to a market agriculture based on wage labor.[37] How this class will interact with and influence the democratic policies of the state is a question that one must wait for time to answer.

In Pakistan, too, a whole new class of small entrepreneurs has emerged along with the speed of higher education. "Pakistan in the 1980s and 1990s is beginning to go through the explosive rural economic transformation that adjacent areas of India had experienced two decades earlier."[38] Will such changes erode the traditional privileges of the landowning families of the Punjab or will new social forces consolidate, rather than fragment, tribal and ethnic constituents? The answer to that question may decide the fate of Pakistan's first few hesitant steps towards the making of a civilian democratic order.

7. As we have seen, the Indian state adopted secularism as a creed to give shape to its democratic political order. Such a creed was perhaps unavoidable in the circumstances of a complex plural society. Hindus constitute the great majority but, unlike other religions, Hinduism has no fixed loyalties. Neither has it an organized church or clergy. Besides, Hinduism includes a collection of nationalities with all or most having a separate language, history and culture. In such a situation, domination of one group over others has been impracticable. Secularism, therefore, was essential for laying the foundation of a strong state. This did not debar the state from associating itself with religious affairs: it patronized all religions equally, at least until the arrival of overtly Hindu movements. In its linguistic policies, too, the Indian state showed caution. Although Hindi, which is the language of one-third of the population, was made the national language, care was taken in response to local demands to reorganize "provinces" on the basis of a linguistic majority. The solution was not foolproof, but "the changes that India has made in its political map have preserved the essential unity of the nation, rather than contributing, as many predicted, to a process of balkanization."[40]

Such a policy of cultural polytheism is absent in other South Asian countries. Instead of keeping aloof, the state has identified itself with the religion and language of the majority. In the case of Pakistan it was perhaps unavoidable, since the claim for a separate Muslim state was made on the basis of religious affiliation of a particular community. It was natural for Pakistan to declare itself an Islamic Republic. Even so, there has been no yielding to the Mullahs to run the state on the lines of Ayatollah Khomeini. As Zia once said 'as Judaism was essential to Israel, so was Islam for Pakistan'. The danger comes from the emphasis on homogeneity in one sphere spilling over into other spheres. Islamabad's attempt to impose Urdu on the Bengalis fanned the flames of Bengali nationalism. In Sri Lanka the pursuit of a trinity of one people, one language and one religion has split the island on ethnic lines. It seems, therefore, to be the case that tolerance of cultural pluralism must be an essential precondition for the growth of democracy.

8. Here, paradoxically, we should note that the centrality of India's role in the region has determined the political behavior of its neighboring states. In many ways, all societies in South Asia constitute parts of a single cultural mix. Pakistan's Islam is but a product of the Indian subcontinent; Hinduism and Buddhism took root in the Indo-Gangetic plain. Linguistically, Bangladesh is an extension of the neighboring state in India. Yet, as Abeyesakara puts it, "recent facts illustrate that the role of the Indo-Gangetic valley as an originator of much of South Asian culture can in itself be a hindrance rather than a motivation to forms of current cooperation."[41] It is by distancing themselves from India that other nations of South Asia gain a psychological confidence about their sovereignty. As they see it, India's economic and military power poses a threat to their own security and an undercurrent of fear about India and its intentions guides their domestic and external actions. The Bangladeshi is never tired of telling that, in 1971, Indian tanks entered Dhaka within less than fourteen hours. The Nepalese acknowledge India's part in pulling down the Rana oligarchy only to remind themselves that India could repeat the feat at any time in the future. In Sri Lanka, one witnessed the regrouping of both Tamils and Sinhalese to secure the withdrawal in March 1990 of the Indian Peace Keeping Force as an "army of occupation."

Hence, India's position as a regional power—and as something less than a full democracy—has tended to push its neighboring states into an opposite direction. This is not to suggest that democracy, unlike revolution, cannot be exported, but for all the states on India's borders, security has become as important as the achievement of popular freedom. In a peaceful world, democracies would live in harmony with democracies, but South Asia is very far from being a peaceful subcontinent, and security as an aspect of an imperfect democracy remains, as yet, an unexplored subject. We would do well to study this before condemning, out of hand, the non-democracies of the Third World.

NOTES

1. Of 126 countries (1982), Pakistan ranked 101. Sri Lanka 104, India 116, Nepal 123 and Bangladesh 125. Maldives and Bhutan had per capita income of less than $170.
2. Lloyd Rudolph and Suzanne H. Rudolph, *In Pursuit of Lakshmi,* (Bombay, 1987), 4.
3. For a brief survey of the Tamil-Sinhalese conflict see Dennis Austin and Anirudha Gupta, *Lions and Tigers: The Crisis in Sri Lanka* (London, 1988).
4. Hamza Alavi, "Class and State in Pakistan" in D. Banarjee, ed., *Marxian Theory and the Third World* (Delhi, 1985).
5. The term used by the Rudolphs, no. 2, 398.
6. *Ibid.,* 400.
7. Urmila Phadnis, "Sri Lanka: Crisis of Legitimacy and Integration" in Larry Diamond, no. 4, 164.
8. See Anirudha Gupta, "Post-Election Politics in Nepal", *International Studies* (New Delhi) vol. 24 (no.2), 91-100.
9. "The prospects of transforming the plurality of numbers into real economic gains for the poor are made very slim by layers of obstacles at the ideological, organizational, electoral, governmental and bureaucratic levels. Substantial success, if achieved, tends to undermine the stability of the democratic system," Atul Kohil, *The State and Poverty in India: The politics of Reform,* (Cambridge, 1987), 45.
10. It was only in 1986 that differences between President Zail Singh and Prime Minister Rajiv Gandhi took a serious turn. however, things settled with the retirement of President Zail Singh.
11. Phadnis, no. 11, 163.

12. In addition to a Presidential System, the 1978 Constitution also introduced proportional voting, which was put to use for the first time in the 1989 parliamentary elections.
13. *Economic Political Weekly* (Bombay), August 20, 1988.
14. See Appendix II.
15. See Appendix II.
16. *Regional Studies* (Dhaka), Spring 1985, 52.
17. See "Introduction" in Larry Diamond *et al.*, eds., *Democracy in Asia*, New Delhi, 1989, 4.
18. The Soulbury Commission overruled the Tamil demand for a 50-50 percent sharing of legislative and executive power with the 70 percent Sinhalese. "The Tamils", according to Tilak Gooneratne "had failed to realize that Lord Soulbury had no option but to refuse to enshrine the cancer of communalism by law and that there was no place for communal electorates in the Westminster model of democracy." "The present situation in Sri Lanka" *Asian Affairs* 17 (1), February 1986, 33-45.
19. See K.M. de Silva, *A History of Sri Lanka*, 1981.
20. *Ibid.*, 546.
21. For the text of the Accord see S. Kumar, ed., *Yearbook on India's Foreign Policy 1987-1988* (Delhi, 1988), 233-237.
22. The concept of "Political Culture" appears too ethnocentric to be of any use for social scientists.
23. Leo Rose, "Pakistan: Experiments with bureaucracy", in Larry Diamond, no. 4, 113.
24. The objective resolution, adopted by Pakistan's Constituent Assembly in 1949, emphasized the rejection of the idea of the clergy (Ulemah) being the ultimate sacred authority. However, it stressed the importance of Islam as the ideology of Pakistan, an important criterion being that the head of the state must be a Muslim.
25. Rose, no. 4.
26. *Ibid.*, 113.

27. For these elections see John Bray, "Pakistan in 1989: Benazir's Balancing Act," *The Round Table* (London), vol. 310, 192-200, 1989.

28. See "1978 President election in Bangladesh, A Review", *Asian Affairs* (Dhaka) April-June 1986, vol. 8(2), 31-44.

29. *Keesings Contemporary Archives.*

30. According to Leo Rose, "Political behavior patterns in Bhutan are difficult to relate either to a traditional/feudal or to a modern/secular framework. Nor does Bhutan appear to be in a clear transitional period from one to the other stage," *The Politics of Bhutan* (Cornell University, 1977), 106-107.

31. See Anirudha Gupta, *Politics in Nepal* (Bombay, 1965).

32. *Ibid.*

33. S. Bastian, "Two Elections," *The Thatched Patio* (Columbo), April 1989.

34. *Ibid,* p.20.

35. Rudolphs, no. 2, 400.

36. A Jeyaratnam Wilson, *The Break-up of Sri Lanka* (London, 1988).

37. Rudolphs, no. 2, 54.

38. Rose, no. 4, 134.

39. To his Chief Ministers (April 1, 1950), Jawaharlal Nehru wrote, "I shall not allow communalism to shape our policy nor am I prepared to tolerate barbarous and uncivilized behavior," Nehru, *Letter to Chief Ministers 1957-64,* (Delhi, 1986), 61.

40. J.E. Schwartzberg, "Factors in Linguistic Reorganization of India," in Paul Wallace, ed., *Region and Nation in India,* (New Delhi, 1985), 177.

41. C. Abayesekara, "Asian Cooperation: A Sri Lankan Perspective," *Strategic Studies Series 3,* Kathmandu, 1985, 152-162.

APPENDIX I

Basic Indicators

Country	Population (1986 Millions)	% of population below poverty level		GNP per Capita (US$) 1985	% of literate adults		% of government expenditure on		
		Urban	Rural		Male	Female	Health	Education	Defence
Bangladesh	103.9	86	86	150	43	22	2.0	4.0	—
Bhutan	1.4	—	—	160	—	—	—	—	—
India	772.7	40	51	270	57	29	2.4	1.9	18.8
Maldives	—	—	—	—	—	—	—	—	—
Nepal	16.9	55	61	160	39	12	5.0	12.1	6.2
Pakistan	102.9	32	29	320	40	19	1.1	2.9	32.3
Sri Lanka	16.5	—	—	380	91	83	3.6	2.4	2.6
Source: 1989 *Third World Almanac*, Oxford									

APPENDIX II

National Elections: India

	1952	1957	1962	1967	1971	1976	1980	1984	1989	1991
Electorate (Millions)	171.7	193.7	216.4	249	274	321	356	489	489	492
Voter turn out (%)	46	47	55	61	55	60	57	63	58	55
Congress % of vote	45	48	45	41	44	34.5	43	48	39.5	37.3
JD % of vote	—	—	—	—	—	—	—	—	17.8	10.8
BJP % of vote	—	—	—	—	—	—	—	—	11.4	19.9
Seats Won: Congress								401	197	225
Seats Won: JD								—	143	55
Seats Won: BJP								—	85	119
Source: Government of India, Press Information Bureau										

APPENDIX III

Summary Data on Sri Lankan Elections

Year	Winning Party	Seats Won (% of seats contested)	% of total votes cast
1947	UNP	42 (44.2)	39.80
1952	UNP	54 (56.8)	34.08
1956	MEP + SLFP	51 (53.7)	39.96
1960 (March)	UNP	50 (33.1)	29.62
1960 (July)	SLFP	75 (49.7)	33.59
1965	UNP	60 (43.7)	38.93
1970	SLFP (UF)	90 (60)	36.63
1977	UNP	140 (83.3)	50.9
1988 Presidential	UNP	Premadasa	27.4
1989 Pal.	UNP	—	30.4

CHAPTER 7

THE PROSPECTS FOR DEMOCRACY IN SOUTHEAST ASIA

W. Scott Thompson

The resurgence of democracy—or what bears some of the forms of Western democracy—in the Third World in the 1980s was notable in coming at the end of a long period of declining democratic prospects. It surprised most observers. Even those who had been most sanguine at the political prospects of the successor states of Asia and Africa in the 1950s and 1960s had little hope by 1980, especially after the emergency in India showed that even that most durable and largest of democratic states could put aside its traditions. If, however, India were able to return to the faith, it was also clear that a comparable renaissance could happen elsewhere.

Southeast Asia might have been the region where the early optimists had the greatest reason to lack hope. The war in

Vietnam, lost to totalitarian forces in 1975, had led in its final stages to the imposition of martial law in other Asian states which were unsure of their security as America began its withdrawal: both Presidents Park[1] and Marcos of South Korea and the Philippines attributed their new regimes of 1972 to that fact.[2]

Yet the picture was never so grim, and the brighter prospects that developed for democracy in the 1980s had roots from the earlier era. The Vietnam disaster did not have the reverberations anticipated. States in the region had begun to discount the *débacle* in advance. Thailand, for example, had drawn up exhaustive economic plans for converting the US military presence to productive uses,[3] and a student-led revolution in 1973, although snuffed out by a conservative regime in 1976, led to democratic reforms whose effects remain, and which have been amplified through 1994. Malaysia survived its emergency of 1969-1971 and returned to a quasi-democratic stability that continues. Indonesians are quick to attribute their own stability and evolving pluralism to the "second chance" which (they acknowledged) the US commitment to Vietnam, despite its ultimate failure, gave to their country.[4]

My argument, however, is that Southeast Asian states have been more idiosyncratic in their movement toward democracy than those of Latin America and Africa and less subject to systemic forces at work worldwide. But if that is true of the past, it may not be so of the future. The further development of democratic institutions in that region will depend on a continuation of the favorable economic climate throughout East and Southeast Asia. Hence, our later argument that systemic *economic* forces will be critical in the future.

MALAYSIA AND THAILAND

There are many possible taxonomies for the successor states of the European empires and their political systems. In Africa, for example, the alternation of francophone and

English-speaking states provides a starting point. Professor Dennis Austin has placed democracies along a spectrum, with Western examples at one end, the fledgling systems somewhere in the middle, and the mixed systems, combining some elements of representative government with authoritarian leadership, further away.

In Southeast Asia there is none of the relative neatness of Africa. We have examples of almost all points on the spectrum. Arguably, Malaysia, which has thirty years' experience of parliamentary government, comes closest to the western model, an achievement which is all the more impressive given the plural and geographical challenges that the federation has faced. As Larry Diamond has said, "The brief experience and haunting fear of a violent ethnic convulsion led in Malaysia to a political restructuring in which competition was limited and fixed to produce a firm parliamentary majority for the Malays and hegemony. While this restructuring has leveled parliamentary democracy down to a semidemocratic status, it has also brought considerable ethnic peace, political stability and socioeconomic prosperity."[5] That was borne out in the October 1990 elections when the ruling Barisan Nasional (National Front) coalition was returned to office, although with a reduced majority of 127 seats in the federal parliament of 180 members. In the election, Tengku Ahmad Rithauddeen (defense minister) and Datuk Amar Stephen Yong (science minister) lost their seats in Kelantan and Sarawak.

One must note of Malaysia that the British inheritance has been critical: almost all of the Third World democratic success stories—at least those of long duration—are former British colonies. If the present prime minister, Dr. Mahathir Mohamad, in office since July 1981, seems bent on weakening that inheritance, there are countervailing forces at work in the federation which limit the amount of change he can induce—a strong bureaucracy, vital traditional centers of power, and a sense of legitimacy among the voting public for the instruments of democracy.

LIBERAL DEMOCRACY IN NON-WESTERN STATES

One can hardly discern the long-term patterns or prospects for Singapore and Indonesia, given the past domination of their respective leaders whose successors have to create, in vastly different circumstances, power bases amid competing elites. But it can surely be said of Indonesia that, below the highest level, a more plural society is evolving in which elections and the circulation of elites are accepted and well used. In Singapore, Lee Kuan Yew tendered his resignation in November 1990 after 31 years in office. He was succeeded by Goh Chok Tong of the People's Action party. Elections followed at the end of August 1991 when the opposition Democratic party increased its single seat to four against 77 for the PAP.

The Thai case deserves more careful consideration. Clearly at this point it is a mixed system, combining a (partially) elected parliament, competing parties, and which included an unprecedented ten-year record of peaceful transfers of power. The received wisdom is that the most important transition was the student-inspired revolution of 1973 whose democratic goals were far-reaching and systematically thought through. Many of the actors of that event remain active and in positions of influence. Yet *three* other factors are more salient for the future of democracy in the kingdom. Each originates from the 1973 overthrow of the Thanom-Prapat dictatorship.

First is the role of the palace, as His Majesty King Phomiphon is sacredly, if euphemistically, referred to in Thailand. It was the king who used his available credit to effect the 1973 political transition from military to civil hands. His power has not ceased to grow, but precisely because of the reluctance of Thai observers to discuss 'the palace' foreign observers have generally failed to separate the apparent flourishing of democracy, behind the facade of a parliament in which the military still holds decisive power, from a benign but decisive royal role.[6]

Second, the growing legitimacy of democracy: in 1979, the resignation of Prime Minister (General) Kriangsak Chonomon, following a parliamentary no-confidence vote, was critical. Kriangsak, to wide acclaim, had overthrown a generally unpopular and repressive regime in 1977; but his stepping down in 1979, and making way for General Prem, who was more highly favored in the palace, was a decisive step by the Thai military towards limiting its role in the polity.

The General's 1984 observation that "there would never be another Thai military coup"[7] is somewhat belied by his own alleged participation in a botched coup in 1987, yet the fact remains that military wings were regularly clipped throughout the decade,[8] and the 1988 resignation of Prime Minister Prem led again to a peaceful transfer of power.

The coup d'etat of February 1991 and sucessive events bore out the lessons of 1973 and thereafter. An unpopular general, Suchinda Kraprayoon, threw out an admittedly corrupt but elected government, and then was stunned that his own supposedly figure-head prime minister, the highly respected former diplomat Anand Panyarchun, took his duties and powers seriously, moving the countru decisively toward elections. But Suchinda turned around and insisted, after the corrupt elections of 1992, on naming himself prime minister, though he was manifestly not a serving parliamentarian, as required constitutionally.

Crisis followed crisis until May, when blood was shed, this time in larger quantity than two decades earlier. There was the additional difference in the level of commitment: Thailand now had an educated and prosperous middle class that wanted to be better than what Suchinda offered. Their blood on the Praman parade grounds led to a constitutional crisis, resolved by the King who brought a humbled Suchinda literally to his knees. Back came Anand as provisional prime minister, again taking his duties seriously. To the astonishment of all, he sacked the offenders of the May events—the leading military powers of the kingdom—and then organized election anew. In a meeting the day after these extraordinary events, which presage so much for at least some broadening of democracy in

Thailand, he told the present author that in his observations, countries whose political institutions did not keep up with their economic progress eventually stalemated. Mexico he gave as an example. Thailand, he said, woulf have to modernize politically asa fast as it was minifestly doing economically. In the weeks that followed, emboldened democratic forces sacked the military from many lucrative positions across the kingdom.

Nirvana did not follow. The new government, headed by a respected but weak prime minister, Chuan Leekpai, could only tread water democratically as the military attempted to regain their prerogatives. But what seemed apparent was that the military could never so brazenly thwart the newly empowered middle class as it attempted to do in May 1992. The question was how quickly and how competently this new middle class could ensconce itself alonside the still influential military elite. It was a hopeful sign that young military officers looked to professionalism rather than political patronage and power as the key to their future, as they revealed to at least one interviewer in the aftermath of these events. Thailand had come a long way.

The *third* point is the economic miracle of Thailand, which has made it the newest NIC (Newly Industrializing Country). Prosperity has given Thai leaders leeway to contain the destabilizing forces that have so often provided the pretext for military intervention in the past—for example, the curtailing of subsidies on rice prices in Bangkok, and given them ample funds from a growing budgetary surplus to 'spread the wealth' and buy off discontent.

Historically, the bureaucracy and the military have shared roles and power from the foundation of the Ayuttya kingdom.[9] It was not in accord with five hundred years of Thai tradition for the monarchy to be as weak as it was between the 1932 coup and the 1973 resurgence. Similarly, it was not in line with Thai tradition for the military to be as weak as it was during the brief, purely democratic interregnum of 1973-1976. Nor does democracy have roots in Thai history: but what does persist is the ability to adapt to external influences of which democracy is today a powerful element.

The fusion that has been effected in the Thai polity of a quietly strong monarch, a military with substantial, but since 1992, rapidly diminishing, veto power to protect its corporate interests, and democratic institutions within which the new educated elites now have a voice and substantial influence, is, therefore, well suited to Thai history. Assuming prosperity continues, one might cautiously predict further democratic reforms, and a continued diminution of military power, but down only to a critical mass. The king's role will continue to operate as long as the ninth reign continues; a problematic succession opens up the possibility either of further democratic evolution or a resurgence of militarism.[10] Thus, one is cautious in assessing the kingdom's democratic prospects.

THE PHILIPPINES

The Philippines is the fledgling state making the widest claims to a full acceptance of the Western model even to the extent of naming its institutions after its American role model. I will argue that the prospects for its success are probably less high, in the medium term, than in Thailand and Malaysia.

A RAND Corporation study in 1969, at a time when democracy was getting a bad name in the Philippines, found statistical support for the notion that it was alive and well.[11] True, elections were corrupt—that of 1969 was historic in that regard—and the same names seemed to circulate in the Senate and House of Representatives with some regularity. But representatives of the people were highly sensitive to public mood, and many undertook systematic polling of elite attitudes in both urban and rural areas.[12] Given how recently the Philippines had emerged from an essentially feudal status, it was hardly surprising that patron-client patterns were sustained within the framework of democracy; indeed it might be argued that their operation was something of a triumph for the latter.

Moreover, in 1986, after fourteen years of an increasingly corrupt dictatorship, the masses of Manila turned out into the streets and peaceably, albeit with the help of the military and the ex-colonial patron who had helped to install martial law,[13] drove Ferdinand and Imelda Marcos from Malacanang Palace. The return to the legality of the pre-Marcos era was swift and effective. It happened in a context of democratic change throughout the developing world which reinforced it and which it helped to reinforce. As a result, a cottage industry sprang up of studies of the Philippines' return to democracy in heroic mold.[14]

There were contrasting data which suggest a different and, ultimately, less optimistic outcome for democracy in the Philippines.[15]

In 1972 Marcos was able to subvert the institutions which had supported local elites for several decades with little or no mass protest. He did it firstly by paying off delegates within what had become an imprisoning constitutional convention and then, with more than a glint of steel, arresting thirty thousand opponents (or suspected opponents) who might be expected to place obstacles in the way of his proposed 'New Society'.[16]

The presumed explanation was that the structural problems of the archipelago—demographic, economic and social—had so overwhelmed the nation that it was willing to accept bold actions to break the hammerlock of the past. But by the end of the 1980s, in addition to the catastrophe which the Marcos regime had brought to the republic, it was increasingly apparent that the new institutions of democracy had shallow foundations which could not withstand the additional demographic, economic and social stress since the coming of the New Society, including seven hundred thousand new job entrants to the economy each year. Moreover, the communist New People's Army (NPA) continued to grow, despite the overthrow of Marcos.[17] By 1989 the NPA was able to operate with varying degrees of freedom of movement in two-thirds of the republic's provinces and had established parallel centers of taxation and governance, reaching even into Manila.

True, Secretary of National Defense Ramos, as he then was, could point to progress by 1991 in bringing the NPA under some substantial measure of control, thanks in large measure to hi own program of reducing military excesses, incentives to the rebels to turn in their arms, along with the generally improved economic prospects of the republic after Marcos's demise. And his presidency brought further progress. But the NPA had been reduced, not eliminated, and as long as the gap between rich and poor remained so wide throughout the archipelago, the NPA or a successor organization—if the NPA were eliminated officially—were likely eventually to spring up and carry the tradition of rebellion on, making the progress of democracy at best uncertain.

It was becoming intuitively obvious—at least to this observer—that the intelligentsia was coming to terms only with the notion of radical change. Reformers were becoming revolutionaries in rhetoric. The evidence mounted of yet another failed land reform.[18] The return of landlords and oligarchy to their old positions in the Senate and House of Representatives[19] where they could once again throttle adaptive change was also not a good omen. Secretary of Trade and Industry, José Concepcion, one of the largest traders and industrialists in the country, was widely believed to have used his enormous power to prevent reform legislation that would open up the economy and put his manufacturing concerns at risk. To this sort of record, an economist simply said, "She [President Aquino] promised liberal democracy. We got it." When it turned out to be 'more of the same' from the earlier era he began paying his dues to the NPA.

Another factor working against the survival of democracy has been the 'coup factor.' The military had historically held a low profile in the archipelago; even today the ratio of defense spending to all government spending, or to gross national product[20] is not unreasonable by regional or Third

World standards. But it was the military that provided the backdrop to the so-called EDSA[21] revolution in which 'people power' was a necessary but hardly sufficient part of the success. The military did not give up this role and its growth in influence continued after President Aquino came to power; she has been helpless to curb its influence, and nearly lost office in the August 1987 and December 1989 coup attempts. The country remained "jittery," in the common expression, about the possibility of further interventions until well into Fidel V. Ramos's accession to the presidency. Whereas in Thailand the use of the coup had been largely routinized and is now downgraded, it is in Filipinos' minds, a new factor, one now never to be discounted.

One illusion many Western students of Philippine democracy sustained derived from the apparent similarity of institutions in that country and in the West, particularly in the United States which had provided the explicit model. A presidency, a senate and a house of representatives hid two more pervasive underpinnings of Philippine politics. One was the Malay basis of the society, a consensus culture which only appeared to be making its political bargains through the institutions of popular power in Manila. It is, in some ways, more instructive to compare Filipino political culture not with the West but with its sister Malay-based state, Malaysia, of which several authorities have argued that "the strong curbs placed on political conflict and dissent may be seen as reflective of Malay cultural values, which appreciate strong authority and fear conflict and dissension."[22]

The other underpinning has been the Spanish heritage. Representatives of the King of Castile held the islands as personal property, like Leopold of the Belgians in the Congo. They were to be exploited and they were: the tradition flourished for almost four hundred years. Notions of individual rights did not develop, not even in the revolution against the Spaniards which Theodore Roosevelt's America so shrewdly exploited. But a form of personalism ironically did develop, in considerable contrast to Malaysia (but not in contrast to Indonesia). It developed as an outgrowth of the mixed ethnic heritage of the ruling elite and the fact that social status among the ruling *meztizos* arose largely from (in David Steinberg's words), "wealth and consumption"[23] as opposed to descent from a pre-colonial elite.

The *ilustrados*—the rich landowners who had collaborated with the Spanish—made their more successful and adaptive pact with a newly powerful United States quickly and crisply. The latter had no experience of imposing colonial rule, had a sense of guilt about the enterprise, and was easily taken advantage of. Like Rex Mottram accepting Catholic instruction in Evelyn Waugh's *Brideshead Revisited*, the elite swiftly learned the litany of American democracy. As long as their sugar quota was protected in the American market, they had plenty of money to sustain their personal rule without any overdue reliance on democratic substance.

There was little evidence, therefore, in the middle of the 1990s that democratic institutions in the Philippines could easliy be sustained. Although economic growth picked up after the 1986 revolution, its benefits were not trickling down to the two-thirds of the country officially below the poverty level. Population growth in the meantime was adding heavily to the social burden, and the will was lacking to try and restructure local values to bring the birthrate into line with resources. Natural disasters brought their own turmoil, placing additional burdens on a faltering government and an undisciplined army. A major earthquake occurred in northern Luzon in July 1990; typhoons and floods have been a constant misfortune. In June 1991 Mt. Pinatubo erupted, bringing a terrible loss of life and property.[24] The Gulf War of 1990-1991 was a further blow, resulting in the cessation of hard currency remittances by the tens of thousands of Filipinos employed in Kuwait. These were unexpected disasters which at least the Aquino government found it painfully difficult to meet. Moreover, the 1992 presidential elections cast a long shadow before the democratic prospects of the Philippines, for there was little sign in the electoral competion that the country had found the democratic institutions needed to resolve distribution issues in a manner which conformed to traditional beliefs, societal patterns and the needs of the poor. In brief, it was not easy to see democracy surviving in any final, lasting form after the momentum of the EDSA revolution, even given the greater stability which President Ramos bequeathed on the land. Only in the long run, let us say after the passage of a half or a full generation, might one look for the striking of a new balance between a revived authoritarianism and a tradition-based democracy, thereby achieving a position somewhere between the present experience of Malaysia and that of Indonesia, both fellow Malay states.

CONCLUSION

We thus have a quilt without patterns for democracy in Southeast Asia. On balance, there are modestly hopeful prospects. The area is prosperous overall. The achievement of the Indochinese settlement removes an obstacle to stability. If the Philippine military does again seize power in Manila, one can be sure that it will be a regime seeking legitimacy in democratic guise and an eventual return to democratic rule. Thailand and Malaysia will continue to maintain strong elements of pluralism, and Indonesia and Singapore have sufficient wealth and adaptive traits for us to be hopeful about their evolution after the legacy of Suharto and Lee Kuan-yu.

We have surely seen in the development of democracy in the West, and in those successful examples in the Third World, the extent to which prosperity is a necessary, if not sufficient, condition for its success. David Potter made the argument long ago for America:

> ...there is a strong case for believing that democracy is clearly most appropriate for countries which enjoy an economic surplus and least appropriate for countries where

there is an economic insufficiency. In short, economic abundance is conducive to political democracy.... A country with inadequate wealth, therefore, could not safely promise its citizens more than security of status—at a low level in the social hierarchy and with a meager living. But this promise is, in its denial of equality, by definition, undemocratic. A democracy, by contrast, setting equality as its goal, must promise opportunity, for the goal of equality becomes a mockery unless there is some means of attaining it. But in promising opportunity, the democracy is constantly arousing expectations which it lacks the current means to fulfill and is betting on its ability to procure the necessary means by the very act of stimulating people to demand and go after them.[25]

The wealth of Japan, the markets of China, and the economic miracles of Malaysia, Singapore, and Thailand provide some margin for error in each of the Southeast Asian states. "To be democratic in adversity is a stern test," Dennis Austin writes in his essay,[26] and how much more so when the traditions are young. But the wars have ended in the region, and the prosperity of Japan and the NICs are beginning to lap over Indochina very rapidly and will certainly keep the Philippines above the status of a banana-republic. But democracy as such will continue to be more idiosyncratic in this region than elsewhere, its success dependent on the discovery of forms and institutions suitable to the history of the respective states and on each government's ability to keep one step ahead of popular expectations.

NOTES

1. Statement made by Ambassador (and then presidential NSC assistant) Dr. K.W. Kim at a seminar, Fletcher School of Law and Diplomacy, October 1972.
2. The fact that such an argument was self-serving does not negate its salience: there was uncertainty about the prospects for stability in a region from which the leading military power present proposed to withdraw.
3. See W. Scott Thompson, *Unequal Partners: Philippines and Thai Relations with the United States*, Boston, 1976, chapter 8.
4. A point made often by the influential head of Indonesia's (semi-official) Center for Strategic and International Affairs, Dr. Jusuf Wanandi.
5. 'Introduction', in Diamond, Linz, and Lipset, *op.cit.* See, too, Gordon P. Means, *Malaysian Politics, The Second Generation*, London, O.V.P. 1991.
6. For a more analytical view, see the unpublished dissertation of Vifarat Isarakdi, "The Men in Khaki: The Role of the Thai Military" Fletcher School of Law and Diplomacy, 1989.
7. Conversations with the present writer, December 1985, Bangkok.
8. See Isarakdi, *op.cit.*
9. See David Wilson's pertinent analysis of the historic foundations of power in the kingdom, *Politics in Thailand*, New York: Cornell University Press, 1962.
10. The Crown Prince enjoys only a tiny portion of his father's prestige because of his widely known and controversial personal behavior.
11. See Rand Corporation, "A Crisis of Ambiguity: Political and Economic Development in the Philippines," by H. A. Averch, F. H. Denton, and J. E. Koehler, 1970.

12. See, for example, Frank Lynch and Peria Makil's PAAS-CU/IPC "Study of Schools and Influentials," Institute of Philippine Culture, Quezon City, 1972.

13. See Thompson, op.cit., 151, for implicit evidence of American support of Marcos's imposition of martial law. It must be recalled that the then dominant force in American foreign policy, Henry Kissinger, shared none of the distaste his successors showed for authoritarian rule among American allies. Not noted in that study was the then American Ambassador Henry Byroade's explicit acknowledgement of his discussions with Marcos of the impact of martial law on US-Philippine relations, in an interview with the author. It was widely and truly believed that the US did not discourage Marcos. See also Raymond Bonner, *Waltzing with a Dictator*, 2nd Edition, New York, 1988.

14. See, for example Lucy Komisar, *Corazon Aquino, The Story of a Revolution*, Braziller, New York, 1987.

15. For a fuller discussion, see the author's *The Philippines in Crisis: Development and Security in the Aquino Era*, New York, 1992.

16. See Karl Jackson's perceptive essay, "The Philippines: The Search for a Suitable Democratic Solution 1946-1986," in *Democracy in Developing Countries: Asia*, Larry Diamond, Juan J. Linz, and Seymour Martin Lipset, eds., Boulder, Colorado, 1989.

17. See Department of Defense, Republic of the Philippines, "Reference Folder of the AFP, 01 March 1988," charts 9-13, data supplied by Secretary of Defense Fidel V. Ramos.

18. Although a land reform act was passed in June 1988, it had been so watered down and was so little, so late, that it was possible for one-time supporters to argue that it would do more harm than good.

19. Not just in the institutions of government. In March 1988 the so-called sugar barons held a convention in Cebu where one of their number, a prominent senator, openly

proposed the bribing of journalists to get them to support their positions.

20. The former was approximately 14%, the latter 2%, not high by comparison with countries of similar size.

21. So entitled because of the location of the principal confrontation between the crowds and the military —the EDSA intersection.

22. Larry Diamond, "Introduction: Persistence, Erosion, Breakdown, and Renewal," in Diamond, Linz, and Lipset, *op.cit.*, 16.

23. Cited in Jackson, *op.cit.*, 235.

24. One result of the eruption was the enforced closure of Clark air base.

25. David Potter, *People of Plenty*, pp.112-115, Chicago, 1954.

26. See above, 22.

CHAPTER 8

THE POSSIBILITY OF LIBERAL DEMOCRACY IN EAST ASIAN SOCIETIES

Benjamin I. Schwartz

The following pages consider the entire "Sinitic cultural area" on the assumption that it is just as legitimate to speak of a common East Asian civilization as it is to speak of a Western civilization. If we can speak of a common Western cultural heritage shared by the nation-state societies of Europe and the Americas, despite the quite separate histories and subcultures of these national societies, it is certainly just as legitimate to speak of a common "Sinitic" culture shared by Taiwan, Mainland China, South and North Korea, Vietnam, Japan, Hong Kong and Singapore, There has, to be sure, been a marked tendency until recently to treat Japanese society as *sui generis* by stressing the more specific features which seemed to distinguish Japan from other East Asian societies, just as there is often a tendency among us to separate off Anglo-

American culture from Western culture as a whole. Yet recent developments, particularly in the realm of economic growth, have tended to turn our attention away from Japanese uniqueness to common East Asian cultural dispositions.

Before discussing the question of the assimilability of liberal democracy (or parts of liberal democracy) by East Asian societies, I look first at some of my own basic assumptions and attitudes concerning political democracy as such. I do not propose a definition of the essence of political democracy and am quite content at this point to list under this heading many factors conventionally associated with the concept—factors such as free, secret and regular elections based on a universal suffrage, representative institutions, competing political parties, and legally secured individual and minority rights. Whether all these features are bound together by indissoluble "necessary relations" is, of course, a matter of endless debate in political theory. As Professor Austin has indicated, it is possible for "parts" of the complex to be present in the absence of other parts. Yet whenever we discuss political democracy as a total political order we tend to include all these parts.

I share the view that the confluence of the ingredients of political democracy first takes place within the Western cultural and social-political sphere, just as the confluence of the ingredients of a fully industrial society also occurs first in the West, although the question of the relationship of these two to each other is enormously complex and by no means totally resolved. I would also add that the failure of other cultures to give rise to these developments is no proof that they are simply at an "immature stage" of a unilinear global human development process which has achieved its full maturity only in the twentieth-century West.

I would add that while I regard "liberal democracy" as one of the most positive and precious heritages of the enlightenment, one of the things I admire most about it is the modesty of its claims as essentially a corpus of "rules of the game."

Unlike words like "capitalism" and "modernization," which bear with them the pretense of total explanatory and soteriological powers, liberal democracy is mainly a political arrangement. It focuses attention on an area where human conscious purposes and decisions—fallible as they are—play a role, a fact which in the view of both vulgar Marxism and of much Western social science reduces its status to the role of "superstructure" or "spinoff" of more "fundamental processes."

I would agree that political democracy, where it exists, occupies a limited area within the total complex of modern societies. It does not explain everything and it certainly does not cure all ills. In my own view of the present spiritual, cultural, social and economic and even political state of my own society, I belong, on the whole, to the company of the critical rather than to the company of the celebrants. While my own personal life is comfortable, and while the present ills of our society may not compare in their immediacy and starkness to the miseries of many other societies (at least for the majority of our citizens), the ills are serious ills which may become worse. None of this, however, diminishes in the slightest degree one's respect for the institutions of political democracy defective as they may be in their actual operation. What the democratic "rules of the game" can provide at their best is an environment of civility, of a minimalization of the role of arbitrary violence and coercion, and the presence of procedures for legislation and judicial action, which one may hope, will continue to yield remedies for some of the evils which afflict us. The term "rules of the game" may seem prosaic and deprecatory but the rules are not self-sustaining. They require the consensus of a majority to support the principles on which they are based in face of ethnic hostility, deep conflicts of interest and passionate differences of belief. The presence of such a consensus, where it is attainable, is an enormous achievement which probably remains more precarious than some think even in some of the "industrial democracies." The writer of these lines is old enough to remember vividly the doubts concerning the survival of the consensus during the great depression even in societies with long-established political democracies. In France, the achievement of a firm democratic consensus has only occurred in recent years; in inter-war years it never caught on in Weimar Germany. Those who now see in the combination of a Western style industrial capitalism and political democracy the irreversible "wave of the future" forget that this phrase was often used in the thirties—with the support of quite sophisticated and convincing arguments—to support both the Stalinist Communist and Fascist reactions against an earlier triumphant liberalism. I mention this recent history of the West here because this history is by no means irrelevant to the entire story of political democracy in the history of twentieth-century East Asian societies.

Indeed, before considering the viability of liberal democracy in East Asian societies, something must be said not only about recent western history but about our assumptions concerning the antecedents of liberal democracy within the long history of western culture. Also, since current western discourse tends to lay stress on the relation between economic development and political democracy, I should like to raise questions concerning some of the more facile assumptions about this matter within the western context. Dennis Austin in his essay remarks that the relationship between economics and politics is seldom simple, an observation that applies as much to the history of the West as to contemporary non-western societies.

Whenever we apply categories derived from the West to non-western cultures we must constantly reexamine the meanings of these categories in the original context of western culture and history. It is interesting to note that there is a vast literature of political theory which continues to discuss the origins of political democracy without relating it to the subject of modern economic development. Thus, however different modern conceptions of political democracy may be from the "direct democracy" of ancient Athens (with all its inbuilt limitations) there is still the view that the Athenian idea of the participation of those defined as citizens in the process of political decision-making has been a necessary precondition for the entire subsequent development of the democratic idea even though the Greek notion that democracy could be realized only within the polity of a city-state may have strongly inhibited all efforts to realize "democracy" in subsequent centuries. It is only in the eighteenth century that a modified interpretation emerges which implies that, in modern large territorial states, democracy can be realized through representative institutions. Again, the ancient Hebrew idea of the supremacy of law and the prophetic strictures on the role of "secular" monarchy also enter as a strain into the entire discussion of the antecedents of the ideas of democracy. The vast medieval discussion of the proper limits of sacred and secular power defined in law may have had no immediate "democratic" implications in medieval Europe but it certainly encouraged that strain of Catholic thought which stressed the notion of popular sovereignty. Again, the medieval notion of the vested rights of estates grounded in law and of deliberative bodies representing estates had no immediate "liberal democratic" implications in medieval Europe and yet was later extensively used against the absolute states of early modern Europe, in the advocacy of individual and group rights. Finally, there is the well-known discussion of the role of the individual conscience in certain strains of Protestantism as a possible source of ideas of freedom of thought and belief. I discuss all these well-known topics among others mainly to illustrate how far one can go in discussing the history of the antecedents of liberal democracy in the West in terms of political practice and theory before referring to modern economic developments.

It is not my aim to deny any relationship between the ascendancy of a market economy and the rise of ideas of political democracy just as one cannot deny some kind of relation between modern rationalism and modern romanticism. A society in which all economic resources and all economic decision-making power are monopolized by a centralized state has no room for any degree of either individual liberty or democracy. Also, as Montesquieu insisted, a society mired in abysmal poverty can not be democratic (although he also insisted that a society given over to commercialized luxury can also not favor the "virtue" required by democracy).

Once one goes beyond such assertions, the subject becomes most complex and I would like to appeal to some of the insights of Max Weber which still seem to me remarkably fresh in their applicability to modern industrialized economies both in the West and in East Asia. I refer here not to the theory of the "Protestant Ethic" which focuses on the role of the individual entrepreneur in the genesis of industrial capitalism (and thus very much stresses a variety of individualism) but rather to the concept of the "rationalization" of modern society as a whole in all its aspects. It is a concept which covers both the emergence of "rational bureaucracy" in the absolute states of early modern Europe and to the functioning of late industrial society as a going concern. In dealing with early modern Europe, Weber, like some others, suggests that despite their "mercantilism" (a notion which already suggests our orientation to the economic), such states helped to create infrastructures such as banking, various financial devices and the idea of large corporate trading companies which were subordinate to the state but devoted wholly to economic goals. In many ways they provided the prototype of a modern corporation. What is more, some of those absolute states systematically encouraged technological innovation. Whatever the role of individuals in establishing factories and corporations, what they create are huge organizations which require the same division and specialization of labor, the same emphasis on hierarchy, status, organizational discipline and clear lines of authority which Weber discerned in the organization of state bureaucracy. While modern corporations may operate within a competitive market economy, Weber did not confuse them with the village blacksmith. Here, indeed, we confront some of the profound ambiguities surrounding the word "capitalism." While Thomas Jefferson undoubtedly believed in private property, and in the free market as it operated in the commercial and agricultural economy of his time, we know that he viewed the emergence of industrial revolution in England with enormous apprehension concerning its implications for democracy as he understood the term. Max Weber, himself, to the extent that he remained a liberal at the end of his life, regarded constitutionalism, parliamentary politics and party politics as ways of confining and controlling the overwhelming tendency toward the universal bureaucratization of modern societies. This may have been an excessively pessimistic view of the situation but at least points to a much more real and complex view of the relations between political democracy and all the disparate phenomena which have come to be shoved into the box called "capitalism."

In dealing with the West, it should of course be obvious, but is nevertheless worth repeating, that antidemocratic tendencies of practice and thought have been very much present from the outset, assuming some of their most extreme manifestations in the twentieth century. In Athens, "direct democracy" confronted the critique of Plato which has exercised a profound influence ever since. Whatever may have been the factors of medieval culture pointing toward democracy, the feudal aristocracy as such was not notably more "democratic" in its inclinations than aristocracies elsewhere. The absolutist bureaucratist states of the early modern age drew on their own theoretical supports. The enlightenment itself was by no means unequivocally committed to the liberal democratic strain. While the *philosophes* were unquestionably committed to the liberty of thought, the "social engineering" beliefs of many of them inclined them much more to the notion of "enlightened despotism" than to the notion of sharing power with the abysmally unenlightened masses. Jacob Talmon and others have demonstrated quite convincingly that the Rousseauist-Jacobin strain of the enlightenment had profound implications for both left and right totalitarianism. While the October Revolution indubitably grew out of Russian social and political conditions, the genealogy of its Marxist-Leninist doctrines is unquestionably Western. I would even maintain that much of Mao Tse-tung's cultural revolutionary rhetoric may owe more to ideas to be found in Robespierre's speeches than to Confucian culture.

Finally, the relationship of modern western nationalism to democracy remains highly ambiguous at best.

I stress this entire range of complexities and tensions within the modern West because it seems highly misleading simply to speak of the response of East Asian culture to "liberal democracy" as an isolated complex. When the articulate political and intellectual elites in East Asia first came into contact with political democracy, they found that it was enmeshed with a host of other factors mentioned above, including differences between the national cultures of Spain, Portugal, France, Holland and England. What these elites confronted in the first instance in their contacts with the West was, of course, not democracy but the unaccountable military, technological and economic ascendancy of these foreigners. Their attention was thus forcibly drawn to what is referred to in the ancient Legalist phrase as the problem of "enriching the state and strengthening the military." Since in the case of both the Chinese literati-official class and the samurai class in Japan, the culture of the past had equipped them with a profound sense of their own vocation and right to rule, they confronted the western threat with a particularly keen awareness of the need to assure the survival of their own polities. Thus both in Meiji Japan and in early twentieth- century China we find groups of people anxious to seek out the secrets of western "wealth and power" whether these were institutional or even intellectual.

LIBERAL DEMOCRACY IN EAST ASIAN SOCIETIES

Much has been made of the slow response of the Chinese elite in the nineteenth century but the fact is that by the beginning of the twentieth small groups of Chinese were eager and willing to seek out the "Wisdom of the West" wherever it might lead, particularly as this wisdom related to technico-economic development and "nation-building." There were also some who, in the nineteenth and early twentieth centuries, were already prepared to find in ideas of political democracy a fundamental source of the West's (particularly Great Britain's) Promethean dynamism. To be sure, this instrumental view of political democracy was in fact mortally vulnerable to any seemingly convincing demonstration that there were more dynamic and effective ways to achieve the goals of modernization. Hence, any commitment based solely on this instrumentalism would certainly remain fragile and precarious. It would, nevertheless, be quite unfair and untrue to say that all those who expressed an enthusiastic commitment to various aspects of political democracy in Meiji or post-Meiji Japan or in early twentieth-century China were adherents of the instrumentalist view.

Before discussing the relation of political democracy to the cultural traditions of East Asia, it may be important to introduce here a contingent factor that has its own considerable weight. It is a historical factor which in the first instance concerns the history of the modern West rather than the history of East Asia. The fact is that after World War I and beginning with the October Revolution we have the beginning of a long and major reaction both by the Communist left and later the Fascist right against the claims of political and economic liberalism to represent the "wave of the future." It was a reaction which was indeed to have a devastating effect on the instrumentalist commitment to political democracy among all those within the articulate elites of East Asia who had thoroughly assimilated the western doctrine of inevitable historic progress. If the Chinese communists were deeply persuaded by the Marxist-Leninist analysis and later the "success" of the Stalinist model, many in the Kuomintang in the years after 1927 were most fascinated with the visions projected by Mussolini and Hitler and came to share their views of the "decadence" of the western liberal democracies. The "radical right" in the Japan of the thirties were also vastly encouraged by the faith that their slogans were as much in line with the direction of global history as they were with the imperial "kokutai."

I am not asserting here that, were it not for this turn in the history of the West, liberal democracy would have triumphed in East Asia. The large social, political and historic factors which led to the failure of constitutional democracy in China of the 1911 revolution were crushing in their weight despite the presence of a tiny intelligentsia open to various "liberal" ideas. In Japan, where some parts of a program of constitutional democracy had actually been realized in the Meiji and Taisho periods, the western liberal influence had a more real impact on the society. However, the militant nationalism which had already been such a decisive and central part of the Meiji revolution from the outset, when confronted with the economic depression and challenges to Japan's imperial destiny in the thirties, certainly no longer favored the particular combination of liberalism and nationalism which had emerged in the Meiji period.

The larger question, however, is the relationship of the enduring and dominant cultural orientations and dispositions of East Asia to the actual history of its societies in the twentieth century. In the case of mainland China, we can go on at great length about the resonance and continuities between Marxism-Leninism-Maoism and certain major orientations of traditional culture and the traditional polity. Certainly many of the student demonstrators in Tianamen Square would have emphasized this "negative continuity." Can one say, however, that Chinese culture was the "cause" of Communist victory in 1949? It may have "unconsciously" influenced the early leadership of the movement (*consciously* they, for the most part, rejected the culture of the past) but the victory of the Communists must be explained in terms of factors operating within the contingencies of recent history—factors such as the failures of Kuomintang policies, the victory within the Communist party of the Maoist strategy of revolution and the massive Japanese assault on China in the thirties and forties—rather than in terms of unchanging cultural continuities. Certainly in the course of the history of the Peoples Republic during the last forty years we find numerous resonances with the authoritarian tradition of the past, with bureaucratic styles and even with the notion of the state as the source of the moral and spiritual authority. On the level of the masses, however, one finds deep continuities with the popular culture of the past, continuities which the regime was determined to suppress. At the same time, there is much in Marxism-Leninism which represents striking departures from the past and which can be understood only in terms of antidemocratic doctrines whose origins can be found only in the West.

While the tendency to see in Chinese Communism a modern projection of the culture of the past remains very popular, there is another current discussion among western scholars concerning the relations of East Asian cultural dispositions to "modernity" which moves in quite a different direction. It centers not on mainland China but on other modern East Asian societies such as Japan, South Korea, Taiwan, Hong Kong and Singapore, and on the spectacular economic development which has, in varying degrees, occurred in recent years in all these societies. What is involved is a major reassessment of the relationship of traditional East Asian culture—which many identify with "Confucian culture"—to the whole process of economic modernization. So long as Japan was regarded as a unique case one could always emphasize the specificities of Tokugawa feudalism in explaining Japan. Yet successes of these other East Asian societies have reminded us again most forcefully that whatever the institutional differences of the Tokugawa period, it was nevertheless the period in which "Confucian culture" reached the height of its development in Japan (some Tokugawa Confucianists were indeed deeply convinced that the Japanese system was much more purely "Confucian" than the contemporary Chinese system). In any case, the notion, so widely accepted in the past, that the Confucian tradition or Chinese culture in general was a major barrier to economic development has now come under serious challenge.

My tentative views on this matter are that, while the overall orientation of traditional Confucian culture was not indifferent to economic matters, it was not in fact oriented to the systematic concentration of human energies on economic development. To the extent that Japan after Meiji, South Korea, Hong Kong and Singapore have made a "societal decision" as it were, to focus their energies on economic development, this decision was not "caused" by the Confucian tradition any more than the Communist victory of 1949 was "caused" by the "despotic" political culture of the past.[1] Here again, one can assert that many attitudes and dispositions of behavior fostered by Confucian culture have proven to be most favorable to the enterprise of development once the project was underway. Among the dispositions frequently mentioned are the emphasis on and extraordinary respect for education and the readiness to submit to organizational and group discipline. Given the traditional emphasis on the economic fortunes of the family (an institution which Talcott Parsons considered an obstacle because of its stress on an "ascriptive" rather than "achievement" orientation), the family in modernizing East Asia has in fact proven to be both ascriptive and achievement oriented. It has actively encouraged the individual ambitions of its members within the larger society.

If we turn from the culture of the past as it effects the dispositions of the individual to some features of the large economic and political order, we again find some facts which do not correspond to our more simpleminded stereotypes.

While it is true that the social status of merchants was low, the Chinese and Japanese economies of the later traditional period were by no means command economies. By and large, the market ordinarily played a leading role in the commercial economy. In China there was a considerable rise in commodity production and internal trade even in the agricultural economy. Private property in its ideal-typical "Lockean" sense was not achieved, but land could certainly be bought and sold. To be sure, the economic sector enjoyed no legally protected autonomy against state intervention and the state certainly did intervene in the economy on various levels for purposes which we might now consider to be both rational and irrational. East Asian societies, where they did not succumb to some rigid western ideological stance as the Chinese communists did after 1949,[2] emerged from the cultural past without clear-cut presuppositions about pure "centralized planned economies" versus the role of "collective organizational" factors. At this stage in their development towards advanced industrial societies, they may in fact enjoy a degree of openness and flexibility concerning the question of the relationship of government to economy (relations which assume a wide variety of forms) and of individual entrepreneurship to the needs of group discipline and cooperation (a relationship often imbued with a strong paternalistic dimension) which the rigid western adherents of the "pure free market and economic individualism" cannot abide.

What then of the relationship of East Asian culture to the possibility and viability of political democracy? It is noteworthy that much of the recent discussion concerning the relation of culture to economic development has tended to overlook the question of political democracy. Those who believe that political democracy is an inevitable "spinoff" of a developed economy may, of course, be highly optimistic about the democratic prospects of the "East Asian dragons." Until recently, however, with the notable exception of Japan, where the emergence of a fully liberal democratic constitution might be explained as an imposition of the American occupation (although this hardly explains its continuing viability) economic development had not led to any full-scale political democracy. Most recently in Taiwan and South Korea the movement to implement constitutional "rules of the game" has been most remarkable. In Singapore with its "dirigiste" capitalist economy we still have a kind of enlightened despotism and in Hong Kong, where an essentially apolitical population enjoyed personal liberty, it seemed until just yesterday willing to forego democracy. Yet here also we note a remarkable shift in attitudes.

Thus, as we have observed, in Taiwan, South Korea, and since the recent events even in Hong Kong and on the mainland itself, there has been an enormous surge in the demand for political democracy in all its aspects. In Taiwan and South Korea we have even witnessed what has thus far been a positive response to these demands. Is this indeed simply the by-product of a mature economy? Is it perhaps based on the fact that both governments and the articulate section of the population are now convinced by the decline of Marxist-Leninist Communism and the teachings of western social science that political democracy is, after all, the true "wave of the future"? Or on the other hand, is it possible than when intellectuals and students in Taiwan, South Korea and in Peking call for democracy, what they are expressing is not so much a deep love for the "rules of the game" as a yearning to remove the present corrupt holders of power in order to replace them with a government of the wise and the pure (a yearning which would certainly be in line with certain traditional cultural orientations)?

All of these elements may be present to some degree. My own inclinations, however, lead me to doubt the theory of the demand for democracy as simply the necessary consequence of a mature economy. My own readings in the media of both Taiwan and on the Mainland before the recent crackdown, as well as impression derived from personal conversations, lead me to believe that there are, in fact, many East Asians who have genuinely come to cherish both ideas of individual rights and at least some of the "rules of the game" of constitutional democracy. Their constant talk of corruption and the arrogance of the powerful may indeed reflect a traditional disposition of Confucian moralism which constantly attacked corrupt and arbitrary officials. Yet, precisely because of this cultural habit, many of them are now genuinely appreciative of that aspect of western constitutional democracy which attempts to subjugate the corruptions and fallibilities of political elites to the constraints and limits of constitutional rules.

None of these considerations provide us with any power to predict the future prospects of political democracy in any of these societies including Japan. Yet, as in the case of economic development, we might ask ourselves at this point whether one can find any dispositions in the culture of the past which might actually prove favorable to the endurance of political democracy as a going concern. Here, I shall only point to certain aspects of Chinese culture seldom mentioned. In high Confucianism there is, first of all, the long tradition of stress on the concept of individual moral autonomy of the true Confucian gentleman. Since this tradition was very much tied to the notion of sociopolitical obligations it created in at least some portion of the elite what might be called a strong civic culture, and even a culture of resistance (not to mention the tradition of popular rebellion). The civic consciousness enjoyed no legal protection and there is a long history of martyrology of "gentlemen" in China. I would, nevertheless, say that this cultural disposition survived in both the pre-1949 modern Chinese intellectual class and even in the behavior of intellectuals and students in the People's Republic.

In China, the political system, however authoritarian, was in many ways markedly different from the Communist regime. While the state had the authority to intervene in any region of social and cultural life, in fact neither in actuality nor in conception was it heavily interventionist in the modern systematic "totalitarian" sense. The orthodox Confucian preference was in fact for "light government." There were large spaces of *relative* freedom in such areas as economic, religious, and intellectual life. Even on the level of popular culture, as in other areas, brutal intervention occurred but was sporadic and *ad hoc* in nature. While established authority demanded obedience, there was on the whole no felt obligation to believe that the present holders of power actually embodied the highest ideals of Confucian culture. I shall not dwell here on the famous notion of the "Mandate of Heaven" and the notion of justified rebellion. Suffice it to say, that the Jacobin-Communist idea of the party which virtually and immanently embodies the "general will" is much more absolutist in its claims.

To be sure, as Professor Austin has remarked, where and if the complex of political democracy does "take hold," as a whole or in part, in East Asian societies, it will operate in a total cultural context quite different from our own. The economic systems with which it is associated may never turn into full Friedmanesque "free market" economies. The attitudes toward the facts of hierarchy, authority and status may for better, or worse, be much more accommodative and affirmative than ours. As we are well aware, political democracy has nowhere eliminated hierarchy, status and authority but this is a fact which leaves us most uncomfortable and resentful. As a modern westerner who shares many western biases I often find the continued stress in Japan on the ceremonious and even enthusiastic acceptance of hierarchy, status and authority quite irritating. Yet this does not mean that the democratic "rules of the game" are not currently operative in Japanese society. In contrast to our notion that the health of a democracy depends wholly on adversarial conflicts of interests and ideas and the constant defiant willingness to assert one's individual rights against the claims of others, these societies may continue to stress social consensus and social harmony as noble social goals. As has been noted, even in our societies a minimal consensus by the majority concerning the "rules of the game" is absolutely essential. To the extent that acceptance of the "rules of the game" becomes part of the consensual culture in future East Asian societies, one can say it may even be considered a favorable factor. It is nevertheless true that dissenting individuals and dissenting minorities are exposed to much harsher *social* pressures than they are in our society. Yet they may still enjoy the protection of the law. It is incidentally to be noted that there are western theorists of democracy who also envisioned the ultimate good society in terms of consensus and harmony. It is also likely that in an East Asian democracy the total "legalization" of human society may never go as far as it has in our society even though constitutional democracy is inconceivable without a thorough "legalization" of the political order.

The concept of culture put forth in these remarks may seem to some paradoxical. On the one hand, in dealing with the culture of the high civilizations, I seem to stress the importance of pervasive cultural orientations. On the other hand, I also stress that one can never evoke culture as the monocausal determinant of recent history and I even suggest that the relation of culture to specific historic events is to some extent indeterminate. The basic assumptions underlying this view is that while cultures may be marked by certain dominant persistent orientations, they are never unproblematic, impermeable, integrated organic wholes. The dominant orientations by no means prevent the emergence of profound complexities, tensions and conflicts. What cultures create are not integrated harmonies but shared problematiques and in the course of their long complex histories they are often open to influences from outside the cultural sphere. In pre-modern China, the reception of Buddhism from India in the third and fourth centuries A.D. reflected the fact that Buddhism, on its various levels, seemed to offer new solutions to various problems with which Chinese were already concerned. But it was also attractive precisely because it may have raised new questions not central to the dominant cultural orientations. The coming of Buddhism did not signal a total displacement of Chinese culture by Indian culture and the debate about the degree to which Buddhism changed China and the degree to which China changed Buddhism still remains unresolved. I do not wish to press the analogy between Buddhism and "western modernity" too far but it is nevertheless suggestive.

NOTES

1. In the case of the two city-states of Hong Kong and Singapore it has been argued that since the accomplishments of the Chinese in these cities was not the creation of high elites but of merchants and plebeians, what we are dealing with here is not "Confucian culture" but a mercantile popular culture. I would simply remark that many of the attitudes we call Confucian are also ingredients of the popular culture.

2. Marxism-Leninism in China is, as elsewhere of course, not merely an "economic strategy." At its heart, there lies a basic concern with the authority of the Leninist state and its basis of legitimacy. During the last ten years, an effort has been made to detach the basis of legitimacy from the commitment to any specific dogmatic "economic strategy." Yet the recent tragic events in Tianamen Square seem to have led the aged leaders to reconsider how much detachment is possible. Yet as we are now aware, the effort to detach economic strategy from political system is now more vigorous than ever.

NOTES ON CONTRIBUTORS

DENNIS AUSTIN is Professor of Government Emeritus, at the University of Manchester, who lives in Macclesfield, United Kingdom. He was lecturer at the University of Ghana (1950-1957), Reader in Commonwealth Studies at the University of London (1957-1962), and Research Fellow at the Royal Institute of International Affairs in London (1962-1967). His major publications include: *Politics in Ghana* (1964), *Britain and South Africa* (1966), *Malta and the End of Empire* (1971), *Ghana Observed* (1974), *Politics in Africa* (1976), *South Africa 1985* (1986), and *Commonwealth and Britain* (1988).

KEITH PANTER-BRICK taught at the London School of Economics from 1950 until retirement in 1985. He was Associate Director of the Institute of Administration in Zaria, Northern Nigeria (1965-1967) and visiting lecturer to several African Universities in Zambia, Zimbabwe and Cameroon. He was editor of *Nigerian Politics and Military Rule* (1970) and of *Soldiers and Oil* (1978). His most recent publication is *Prospects for Democracy in Zambia* (1994).

PAUL CAMMACK is Professor of Politics at the University of Manchester, United Kingdom.

ANIRUDHA GUPTA is Professor of International Studies at Jawaharal Nehru University, New Delhi, India. He is an expert on African and South Asian Affairs. His publications include *Politics in Nepal* (1964), *Indians Abroad: Asia and Africa* (1971), *Government and Politics in Africa* (1975), *Revolution by Ballot: India's 1977 Election* (1977), *Politics in Africa* (1988), *Minorities on India's West Coast* (1993); and co-authored with Dennis Austin *Lions and Tigers: A Study of Tamil Sinhala Conflict* (1988), and *Politics of Violence in India and South Asia: Is Democracy an Endangered Species?* (1991).

SAM C. NOLUTSHUNGU is Professor of International Relations and researcher at the Frederick Douglass Institute at the University of Rochester, New York.

ANTHONY J. PAYNE is Professor of Politics at the University of Sheffield, United Kingdom. He is author of many books and articles in politics in the Caribbean and in small states generally.

BENJAMIN I. SCHWARTZ is at the Center for East Asian Research at Harvard University in Cambridge, MA, USA.

W. SCOTT THOMPSON is the author of *The Philippines in Crisis: Development and Security in the Aquino Era* (1993) and of numerous other books and articles on Asian and African politics. He served as Associate Director, Policy, United States Information Agency, in the Reagan Administration and as a founding member of the Board of Directors of the United States Institute of Peace. He was educated at Stanford and Oxford Universities, where he was a Rhodes Scholar, and has ever since been on the faculty of the Fletcher School of Law and Diplomacy, where he is Director of Southeast Asian Studies.